THE HUNDRED TALES
OF WISDOM

Tales, anecdotes and narratives used in Sufi schools
for the development of insights beyond ordinary perceptions.

THE HUNDRED TALES OF WISDOM

Life, Teachings and Miracles of Jalaludin Rumi from
Aflaki's *Munaqib*, together with certain important stories
from Rumi's works, traditionally known as
'The Hundred Tales of Wisdom'

Translated from the Persian
and presented by

IDRIES SHAH

THE OCTAGON PRESS
LONDON

Also by Idries Shah

1   Sussex University lectures
2   Geneva University lectures
3   University of California and New School for Social Research lectures.

CONTENTS

RUMI'S CHILDHOOD AND YOUTH

It is related that when the Moulana — Jalaluddin — was only five years old, he used to stand up in his cot in a very disturbed frame of mind — having suddenly seen a vision; visions of spiritual personalities, like Gabriel, the Virgin Mary, Abraham and others. When he was in that state, the disciples of his father used to 'calm him down'. His saintly father Bahauddin Walad confirmed upon him the title of 'One-Fashioned-by-God'. Moulana was born at Balkh (Afghanistan) on the 6th of Rabi-al-awwal in the year 604 A.H.*

Narration: Sheikh Badruddin Naqash Al-Moulawi recounts 'I heard from Sultan Walad that he had seen a writing in the notes of the Saintly Bahauddin Walad in his own celebrated handwriting saying that when Jalaluddin Rumi was only six years of age, he was playing on the roof of his house with some playmates of about the same age. During their games, one boy must have suggested jumping from one roof to another. Moulana is reported to have said that that sort of play was but the game of cats and dogs; and so it was a shame that they should engage themselves in such

*Corresponding to 30th September, 1207 of the Christian Era.

5

inferior playfulness. He cried: "Let us go up to the skies and meet the angels." And, so saying, he disappeared from the sight of his young companions. The bewildered boys raised a hue and cry, and thus all men became aware of the incident. After a few moments, when he reappeared he was pale and a little frightened; and said: "When I was talking to you, a group of men clad in green mantles descended upon me from the skies and bore me up into the heavens up above and took me around celestial spaces, and I heard the hue and cry of you boys over my flight, and these creatures brought me back to you." Even at that early age, like many saintly people, he used to eat only once in three or four days or once during the week.'

Another narration has it that the Saintly Bahauddin Walad, Moulana's father, used to say that his son 'is of high parentage, a true Prince, because his grandmother Shumsul Aimma was the daughter of Shumsuddin Sarakhsi, a Sayeda (descendant of the Prophet Mohammed) whose lineage connects her with the Fourth Major Caliph Syedna Ali; and his mother was the daughter of Khwarazm Shah, the King of Balkh; and the mother of my grandfather (Bahauddin's) was the daughter of the King of Balkh.' Thus, it is that both in the material and spiritual senses, he (Moulana) had high connections.

Another narration has it that Moulana said that he, from the age of seven years, used to recite the verse of the *Quran**
which reads thus:

> Surely We have given you an abundance of good;
> therefore, pray to your Lord and make a sacrifice.
> Surely your enemy is the one cut off from good,

*Chapter 108: 'The Abundance'.

and used to weep a great deal in contemplation thereof, 'until the Lord sent His radiance into my heart and a Voice came to me saying: "In the name of Our Magnitude, O Jalaluddin, from now onwards do not subject yourself to an undue degree of spiritual strain, for the portal of Refulgence has already been opened to you." And I thus render limitless thankfulness, so that I might enlighten those who come into contact with me.'

Verse: My entire being has become like a string of the spiritual lyre since the head of the chord has been touched by the Master's hand: Great obstacles I have overpowered, and have thus made the Path easy to my friends.

THE GREEN-MANTLED FIGURES

It is further narrated that two years after his father died, he hied forth to Syria to complete his training in moral and material lore and this was his first journey to Aleppo, where he stayed in the Seminary known as Halavia. There the disciples of his father came to greet him and attended to his wants. He stayed for a long time in that city. Kamaluddin Adeem, who was the Overlord of Aleppo at the time — a man of considerable piety and learning — became a devotee of Moulana and visited him very frequently. The Overlord was especially attached to Moulana because he knew Moulana to be the son of a great spiritual figure of his time, and also because Moulana was so remarkable in acquiring knowledge. Moulana's teachers used to give particular attention to his lessons, thus the other students in the class used to be envious of Moulana's progress in divine literature.

Another narrative has it that the Head of the College used to complain to the Head of the Administration that Moulana often disappeared from his room at midnight. Kamaluddin the Overlord became distressed by these repeated reports of Moulana's nocturnal disappearances. And he was determined to find out what actually did take place. One night when it struck the hour of midnight, Moulana was seen to come out of the College, and Kamaluddin stealthily followed him. When they reached the city gate, the gateway opened of its own accord, and Moulana, leaving the town, walked unconcerned towards the mosque of Abraham Khalilur Rahman. Kamaluddin then saw a white-domed building in front of him, full of strange figures, who were wearing green mantles. Such people Kamaluddin had never seen in his life. He saw these strange men greet Moulana. Overpowered by this spectacle, the Overlord fainted, and remained in an unconscious condition until the late forenoon of that day. When he recovered, he perceived neither the domed building nor the people who had assembled there at night. Bewildered, he roamed about the desert that whole day until the darkness of the night enveloped him. For two days and nights he continued in that state of mind. As the troops of the Overlord had not seen the Head of the Administration for two whole days, they were obviously anxious about the safety of their master. A search-party was sent out to find him with the clue that he had made enquiries some days ago at the college about the night-wanderings of Moulana, and had possibly followed Moulana when he went towards the outer gates of the city. Post-haste, the search-party hastened to the city gate and out into the desert beyond, where one of them rode the whole day looking for Kamaluddin. Incidentally he saw Moulana, too, wandering about, and as Moulana already had pre-knowledge of what they looked for, he told them to go towards the mosque of Khalil.

After much searching the search-party found the object of their quest in an exhausted condition — in thirst and prostrate with fatique — and gave him food and drink. Upon his reviving, he asked the men who told them where he was; whereupon he was told the man who had given the indication of his whereabout was Moulana. Kamaluddin said no more of his experiences to his soldiers, and mounting a horse he rode back to Aleppo.

Greatly affected by what he had seen, the Overlord gave a reception in honour of Moulana, which was attended by a great number of people, and those who were the Moulana's adversaries were put to shame. Seeing, however, that a tremendous number of people were being attracted by him, and he desiring no publicity of that large scale, Moulana travelled down to the city of Damascus. As Sultan Azizuddin Rumi Badruddin Yahya had written to Kamaluddin the Overlord of Aleppo inviting the Moulana to his territory, the Overlord received Moulana with great honour. Kamaluddin of Aleppo had also informed the Overlord of Damascus what he had seen of the great spiritual attainments of Moulana, during the latter's stay at Aleppo.

SAYED BURHANUDDIN TRANSMITS PERCEPTIONS TO RUMI

It is narrated also that one day Sheikh Salahuddin, May God be well Pleased with him, said that on an occasion he (the Sheikh) was sitting in the presence of the Saintly Divine Sayed Burhanuddin; and the attitude was of spiritual contemplation; when the Saint said, speaking about Moulana Jalaluddin Rumi, in high praise of Moulana's pre-eminence in the realm of mystic lore: 'When in my days of great glory, when I was the Tutor of the Sultan, more than twenty times having placed the young Moulana on my shoulders, I had ascended to the high skies in the atmosphere of mysticism; and thus he (Moulana) had arisen into such an undisputed stage of occult distinction; and he owes a great deal to me on that account.' When this was reported to Moulana, he observed that 'It was so and a hundred thousand-fold like that in fact. My gratitude to that family is limitless.'

THE MONKS OF CICILIA

It is likewise narrated that Sheikh Sinanuddin Aq-Shahri Kulahdoz — he being a man of considerable spiritual attainments — that when Moulana was on his way to Damascus, the caravan reaching the territory of Sis in Cicilia, they pitched their tents at a place where some odd monks resided and practised the uncanny art of magic; more especially they predicted future events through their magical knowledge and incantations. Through their weird craft they made a large income.

As soon as they saw Moulana, to impress him, they ordered a boy to rise into the air and stand there, between the earth and the sky.

Seeing this, Moulana reclined his head in contemplation. Instantly the boy called down from above that he must be rescued from his lofty position otherwise he would die from fear of the man in devotional thought. The monks called up to him to come down. He said: 'I cannot descend. I feel as if I am nailed here.' Whatever craft of enchantment and spells the monks tried to bring the boy down from the air was of no avail. There up above he remained. The monks, realising that their art was nullified, placed their heads at the feet of Moulana and, asking forgiveness, begged that he might not expose them. Moulana replied that it could not be done unless the formula was recited: 'I bear witness that there is no God but God; and I bear witness that the Prophet Mohammed is His servant and His Messenger.' The boy recited the verse and instantly came down to earth. Seeing this manifestation the monks acted as did the boy, and begged to accompany Moulana in his wanderings; but the Master desired them to remain where they were, and said that they should just send their greetings to him and to pray for him. In this way both the material and the spiritual path were laid before them, and in that isolated part of the world they addressed themselves to the task of doing good to all who came and departed from that locality.

APPEARANCE OF THE
ENIGMATIC SHAMSI-TABRIZ

When, however, Moulana arrived at Damascus, the learned men and others of importance received him with due honours, and lodged him at the Madrasa Muqadasa — the Sanctified Seminary — and he busied himself with attention in acquiring further knowledge of religious lore. He stayed seven years at Damascus. At the time he was forty years of age.

It is narrated that one day Moulana was having a walk in the park of Damascus when he saw that a strange-looking person had appeared from amongst the crowd. Clad in a black felt long coat, and wearing a peculiar type of headgear, he was quite a person apart from the rest of the people. Reaching near Moulana he kissed Moulana's hands and said: 'Oh, thou Assay-Master, fathom and assay me!' In the rush of people, he was lost in the crowd: and he was Moulana Shamsi Tabriz. The Moulana then looked for him, but he was gone.

SAYED BAHAUDDIN'S TEACHINGS

After a while Moulana Jalaluddin journeyed to Roum (Asiatic Turkey) and as he arrived at Qaysaria, the important personages of the place received him with honour. Sahib Isfahani wanted to invite him to his own house, but Sayed Burhanuddin stated that the custom of Moulana was always to stay at a seminary. The number of people seeking enlightenment almost overwhelming Moulana, he took refuge in the solitude of his room. Perceiving this contemplative aspect of Moulana, the Great Divine (Sayed Badruddin) said to Moulana that he should now seek his (Badruddin's) company in meditation and learn the spiritual and occult manifestations from him; for he (Moulana), with the Grace of God should henceforth seek a fatherly saint for that purpose. Moulana, noticing the inner urge of the Great Saint Sayed Bahaddin, sat at the feet of the Master for futher enlightment.

As a first lesson, the Sayed asked Moulana to fast for seven days, but he replied that seven days were too few, he would fast and meditate for forty days and give himself entirely to the contemplative company of that Master Sage, Badruddin, during which time all he ate was a few barley cakes; and he drank but a little water as breakfast. During those spiritual exercises, he saw the mysteries of the unknown regions, confined as he was in his cell of contemplation.

On the completion of the forty days of fast, when Sayed Badruddin, the Saint, entered the cell of Moulana, he saw Moulana deep in thought, his mind roaring, as it were, into the realms of the Nothingness-on-High; for 'WHAT-EVER IS IN THE WORLD IS BUT IN YOUR OWN *SELF* — SEEK IN YOUR *SELF* WHATEVER YOU WANT, FOR ALL IS YOU.'

Having seen Moulana in that state of contemplation, he left Moulana in that condition, and considered that he desired to undertake another fast of forty days. At the conclusion of the second period of forty days, the Saint entered the cell of Moulana and saw him standing at prayer, tears running over his cheeks. The one who was so intensely engaged in devotion did not pay any attention as to whom had entered his cloister. Sayed, the Saint, once again retraced his steps and left the Moulana to complete the third period of his fast of forty days.

Beside himself with fear for the wellbeing of Moulana, Sayed, the Saint, burst open the door of the cloister, raising his voice in alarm. Thereupon the saint saw Moulana emerge from his cell with a smile upon his lips and a serene expression upon his face. His two eyes were two 'rivers of gladness' and he recited: 'See in these two eyes of ours, the reflection of our celestial Beloved — therein see, too, the dance of the image of our Master.'

Appreciating that enlightenment had been received by Moulana in no uncertain degree, the saint embraced him and said: 'You have been the master-thinker in all moral codes of life, as in all spheres of spiritual existence; but now you have attained the secrets of that which is the innermost of esoteric life, a degree of attainment which the saints and divines of yore might well envy; and I am grateful to have seen that you have reached that stage of virtue and purity. He thereupon asked Moulana to embark on a mission of enlightening the people, and to light the torch of divine love in the hearts of the seekers after truth. Thus it was that Moulana started towards Qonia and began his teaching of the occult lore of mysticism. Henceforth he tied his turban like the Arabs, and wore a cloak with wide sleeves; a fashion which had been the custom of the learned men of ancient times.

In course of time the saint Sayed Bahauddin was called up to paradise, and Moulana went to Qasaria to pray for his soul and soon after returned to Qonia. It was at that time, when the Leader of all the Dervishes, Moulana Shamsi Tabriz, appeared for the second time before Moulana.

It is further reported that Moulana Shamsi Tabriz was a disciple in Tabriz of Sheikh Abu Bakr Tabrizi who was a basket-maker. The Sheikh was widely known for his saintly qualities and high mystical perceptions. The great spiritual and mystical attainments of Moulana Shamsi Tabrizi had, however, risen to such a supreme height that Moulana Shams desired to 'fly higher and higher' so that he might reach loftier vistas and greater regions of mysticism. In this quest he roamed the world for years, and he was given the appellation of Shamsuddin the Drifter.

THE VISION OF SHAMSUDDIN

One night he was greatly distressed in mind and raised a cry about his inner urge and plunged into a state of mind provoked by mystical feelings and then he most earnestly prayed: 'O God, show me one of your great saints and lead me to one of those whom you love.' Shamsuddin was thereby informed that the one whom he was seeking was the son of the Leader of the Learned, one Bahauddin of Balkh. 'Show, O God,' prayed Shamsuddin, 'the face of such a person to me.' He was asked what was he prepared to give in thanksgiving; to which replied Moulana Shamsuddin that he was prepared to give his head for it, as he had nothing dearer than his life. A voice came into his mind: 'Go thou to the country of Roum where thou shalt find the object of thy quest.' With fullness of faith and mighty love, Shamsuddin Tabrizi started towards Roum. Some say that he arrived in Roum from Damascus; others allege that he then again returned to Tabriz and thence travelled to Roum.

ASSAYER OF MYSTIC TREASURES

When he ultimately reached Qonia he put up in a room in the Street of the Sugar Merchants. He put an expensive lock on the door of his rented room, and tied the key in the corner of a richly-woven turban, so that people would consider that he was a wealthy merchant. In fact he used to live in another room with only a straw mat, a half-broken earthen pot, and a brick for his pillow; and a measure of a week's-old barley husk he used to soak in water and drink as his only means of sustenance.

Likewise it is narrated that one day when that Leader of the Wise — Shamsuddin Tabrizi — was sitting at the gateway of an inn, he saw that Moulana Rumi, riding on a fleet-footed camel, had emerged from the Street of the Mirror Sellers. Students and men of learning were following the Moulana on foot alongside his camel. Moulana Shamsuddin Tabrizi ran forward and clutched at the bridle of the Moulana's mount and said: 'Oh, thou, Assayer of Mystic treasures, say whether Mohammed the Prophet was greater or Ba-Yazid.' Moulana replied at once: 'No, no, Mohammed the Messenger of God is much greater, for he is the Leader of the Prophets and the Saints;' and quoted the verse:

'Fortunate is our country,
and to sacrifice ourselves is our duty,
the Leader of our Caravan is Mohammed,
the Honour of the world is he.'

But Shamsuddin again asked: 'What does it mean that the Prophet Mohammed said, "Praise be unto Thee, vouchsafe Thy refulgence", and Ba-Yazid said, "Praise be, and my status is great, and I am the king of all kings".'

As soon as Moulana heard this from Moulana Shamsi Tabriz, he came down from his mount, uttered a cry and descended into unconsciousness. He remained in this state for a whole hour, the populace surging around the unconscious sage; and when he regained consciousness he replied to Moulana Shams, saying: 'Ba-Yazid's "thirst" was quenched by only one cup, and his capacity was satisfied by one draught; and the narrow chink in the door of his mind could admit only that little radiance of God; whereas the "thirst" and capacity of the Prophet Mohammed was limitless and (his vehement desire for God's grace) was beyond measure and as the Quran has said: "Have we not expanded for you your breast. . ." thereby greatly accommodating, and the extent of God is most extensive, therefore the urge and desire of the Prophet was infinitely more great than Ba-Yazid's. Of a truth, the "breath of urge of God's love" is created by a great "thirst".' Saying this, Moulana walked back to the seminary with Moulana Shams Tabrizi and went into contemplative retreat in his cloister with him, where they remained in seclusion for forty days; but some say that they remained in a contemplative condition for three months.

It is further narrated that, Moulana said: 'When Shamsi Tabriz asked me that question, a sort of window opened in the crown of my head and a vapour therefrom rose to the skies.'

The result of that impact from Moulana Shamsi Tabriz and his question was that Moulana stopped delivering lectures at the seminary for a while, nor preached sermons for a time; but gave all his time to deep contemplation over the mysteries of mystic lore; and he wrote the verse:

> Like the star Utarid (Mercury) the elements of my being were scattered about; though I sat in repose a while — but when I saw the secret writing on the forehead of the cup-bearer, I became intoxicated, and broke the pens in ecstasy.

THE TABRIZ MASTER DISAPPEARS

It is further narrated that, when this close contact of the two seekers of mystic lore passed all limits, those who were the Moulana's earlier followers became jealous and said 'Who is this newcomer to have so much occupied the time and attention of our Master so long?' So Moulana Shams disappeared. For a whole month people looked for him, but he was not to be found and no one knew where he went. Moulana Rumi had thereafter had made for himself an especial type of hat and a robe which opened all the way in front, and that was the way that ancient sages were clad. He further asked that the viol should have six strings and should have six sides at the base. Previous to that, that instrument had only four sides. In regard to making the viol six-sided, he explained that 'Our viol is six-sided because each side represents one side of the world, and the strings being straight up are in the form of *Alif*, the first of the Arabic letters, and is the first letter in the name "*Allah*" and *Alif* is the spirit of the soul; thus', he added, 'listen to the *Alif* of *Allah* through the strings, if you have an inward ear of the soul, and see with the inward eye of the soul the name of *Allah* in that *Alif* — the straight lines of the strings.'

At this the Lovers swelled to the soulful music and went into vociferous ecstasies: thus, the weak and the strong, the learned, the illiterate, Muslims and non-Muslims, men of all nations and places, converged towards the Moulana's grace and attention and became his devotees and recited mystical poems and sang songs of mystic meaning. So they acted day and night. But those who were jealous and the dissenters from the mystical lore censured these practices and said 'What is this that is going on — a strange manifestation!'

Men of leisure and wealth, and even some from the ranks of royalty, who — because of intense contemplation and occult practices — had left their previous life of luxury, were so affected as to become even demented — to the sight of common people. One prince, on account of the excessive devotional exercises and going into mystical trances, had become outwardly mad and those infidels who had spoken ill of the Prophet became mad in reality. All this was, of course, due to the influence of Moulana Shamsi Tabriz . . . the Prophet had spoken that 'No one can attain the truth of faith in his heart about God, until men of the world style him mad . . .' and when the reality of Reality of the great Moulana became manifest, those who had received the grace of God became his disciples; and those who had erred were left as abandoned ones: Nothing else is for the Godless one but adversity, and it is said, do not disbelieve the virtuous ones, and fear the fearless God-loving ones, because otherwise the patience of such persons will, of a surety, destroy you.

THE SIX APPARITIONS
AND THE FLOWERS

It is narrated likewise, that the wife of Moulana, known as Kira Khatun, who in piety and rectitude was like the Mother of Jesus, reported that 'One wintry day I saw Moulana resting his head on the knee of Shamsi Tabrizi in repose. This I saw through the chink of the door of his cloister; and then I saw that one side of the wall of the room was opened, and six forms of fearful visage entered through the opening and salutated Moulana and placed a bunch of flowers before him. These persons were there until late in the afternoon, and not a word was spoken.

'Noticing the hour of prayer, Moulana made a sign to Shams to pray and to lead the prayer; he, however, said that in the presence of a superior personality he could not do so. Moulana thereupon led the prayer, after which those six persons left the presence after paying high honour.' Kira Khatun further stated that, witnessing these occurrences, she became unconscious with fear and bewilderment. 'When I came to,' she continued, 'I found Moulana had emerged from the room and gave the bunch of flowers to me, saying that I was to keep them with care. I sent a few petals of those flowers to the herbalists to examine. They said that they had never seen such flowers in their lives and asked where they come from, and what was their name. Furthermore, all the herbalists were amazed by the scent, the colour and the delicate texture of those flowers; and as to how it was possible to have such blooms in the depths of winter.'

Amongst such herbalists was one important master-botanist who often went to India for trade, and used to bring articles of great curiosity and wonderment from that country. He said that the flowers were from India; and that they grew nowhere but in that country, towards the southern tip of that country near Sarandib (Ceylon)*; and how had they reached Roum in such freshness and beauty? And he greatly desired to know how they came into that country at that time. Kira Khatun thereupon was all wonderment. Suddenly Moulana appeared on the scene and said: 'Keep these flowers with great care, and do not reveal their secret to anyone, for those Spiritual Leaders who tend the parts of paradise around India have brought the flowers as a gift to you, so that these flowers may impart inner life to you and add honour to your chastity and piety. Praise be to God, be ever watchful towards these flowers, so that no harm should reach that which is like unto your own eyes.'

It is stated that Kira Khatun kept the leaves and petals with the utmost care, expect that — with the permission of the Moulana — she had given a few leaves to Karkhi Khatun, the wife of the Sultan. The virtue of those was that whosoever had a painful eye and rubbed the petals on it was instantly cured. Never did the colour and perfume of those flowers fade, due to the spiritual attainments of the illustrious friends who brought them.

* Now Sri Lanka

THE SPIRITS AND THE LIGHTS

It is also narrated that they had erected a tall pedestal in the house to place a light thereupon; and Moulana always stood there reading the mystical writings of the saintly Bahauddin from the early part of the night until dawn. One night, however, a group of *Jinyan* (genies, spirits), who lived in the house complained to Kira Khatun that they could no longer stand the light the whole night; and feared that the occupants of the house might be harmed by them. This was duly reported to the Moulana by his wife, who did not then say anything. On the third day he informed Kira Khatun that she need fear no longer, since all those who complained to him had become his disciples; and none of his relatives or friends would be harmed in any way.

THE SECRET RIDE TO BATTLE

It is narrated also that there was a Master Butcher, one
known as the celebrated Jalaluddin, who was one of the
oldest disciples of Moulana. He, too, was a man of great
gifts of high humour and affection. One of his diversions
was to buy colts and after training them, to sell them to
high personages. His stable was always full of excellent
horses. It is narrated that once from the Unknown Vistas
news was flashed to the mind of Moulana that a great
catastrophe was about to come to the world. 'For nearly
forty-odd days', he said, 'Moulana used to roam about in
an uneasy frame of mind, his large turban tied to his waist.
At last', continued the Master Butcher, 'one day I saw
Moulana enter my house in a very preoccupied condition,
and I made obeisance, whereupon he commanded that I
should saddle a very fleet-footed horse for him. Three of us
with much difficulty saddling the resisting mount offered
the horse to Moulana; who, jumping into the saddle, rode
fast towards the land of Qibla (southward). I asked
whether I, too, might accompany him, to which he replied
that I must help him with my moral help.

'Late in the evening I saw that he had returned, his
clothes all covered with dust, and that the horse, which had

a mighty frame like that of an elephant, was so greatly tired out that he was weak to an unimaginable degree. The next day', continued the horse dealer, 'Moulana asked for another horse better than the one which he used the previous day and, as on the day before he rode away in great haste and returned at dusk. The horse was quite exhausted, and I did not dare to ask the reason. On the third day likewise, the Moulana came and asked for a horse and as before rode fast and furiously away. When, however, he returned at the time of the prayer of the evening, he sat down in repose and greatly satisfied; and sang:

' "Congratulations, congratulations, O, ye friends of mine who sing — For that dog-of-hell was sent back to hell;" and I, fearing Moulana greatly, could not ask the reason for all that.

'After a few days when a caravan arrived from Syria, we heard that a horde of Mongols had greatly distressed the city of Damascus; and they said that it was Halaku (Hulagu) Khan; who had taken Baghdad by the sword in 1257, and had killed the Caliph, then took Aleppo and converged towards Damascus; and that Munko-Qa rode up to Damascus; and when their troops had surrounded it, the people of Damascus saw that the Moulana had arrived to help the troops of Islam, with the result that they completely overwhelmed the Mongols. The one who gave these tidings cheered us greatly; and with gladness in our hearts we came to Moulana for him to comment on what had happened at the seige of Damascus; and said the Moulana "Aye, Jalaluddin, it is so." '

THE RICH MERCHANT
AND THE DERVISH OF THE WEST

It is also narrated that important companions had reported that at one time a rich merchant from Tabriz arrived at Qonia, and having put up at the house of a Sugar Merchant, asked as to what celebrated divines resided in that city, so that he might go to salute them and kissing their hands gain virtue by their grace; for it is said that when one might go on a journey, at one's destination one should seek the company of a man of virtue. They replied that in their city there were many men of piety and godliness but the most notable amongst them was the leader of the learned ones, by the name of Sheikh Saddrudeen, who had but few to equal him in religious matters and in the lore of the mystics. Some men of learning took him to the house of Sheikh Saddrudeen; and took some twenty dinars' worth of presents to the Sheikh.

When the Tabriz merchant reached the house of the Sheikh, he saw a crowd of functionaries and servants around attending to the wants of the Sheikh. Seeing this, the devout merchant was much grieved and said to himself that he had come to see a Dervish (who has no need of such retainers and superficial show) and not an Overlord. Those who had brought him there stated that that kind of display did not affect the Sheikh, for he had a heart of mystical attainment; rich sweets do not harm a medical man, but are harmful to an ill one.

The merchant, however, entered the presence of the great Sheikh with considerable distaste; and said that despite his donating large sums in charity and giving generously to the needy, he was always in financial difficulties; and asked its reason and remedy. But the Sheikh paid little heed to his question and application, whereupon the merchant returned with a saddened heart from the presence of the Sheikh.

On the second day, he asked if there was 'no other great divine from whose contact I could profit morally and spiritually'; and thus he was told that there was one other man of piety and virtue; and he was Moulana Jalaluddin Rumi, whose ancestors had been men of learning and piety for fifteen generations; and 'day and night he devotes his time to prayer and meditation and a sea of matters of mysticism.' Upon his showing a keen desire to approach such an one, his friends guided him to the house of Moulana and towards his seminary. They tied fifty dinars in the end of his turban, and when they arrived at the residence of Moulana, they saw him immersed in close study. With the 'influence' surrounding Moulana, the newcomers became 'dazed and affected', and the Tabriz merchant, as soon as he set his eyes upon Moulana, was enormously 'influenced' and began to weep.

Moulana said: 'Your fifty dinars are accepted, but those twenty (which were offered to the Sheikh the previous day) are wasted. God's wrath was about to descend upon you; but in His Grace, He guided you to this seminary; and from this day onwards, be of good cheer: no ill-luck will attend to your business.' The merchant was greatly impressed by this message, for he had not spoken his heart's desire yet.

Moulana further said: 'The reason for your misfortunes was that one day you were walking in a street in the regions of the western Franks, and there you saw a great Frank* Dervish sleeping at the crossroads. Disliking his poverty-stricken frame and the place where he slept, you stepped over him, as if disgusted by his misery. The heart of that saintly person was thereby hurt. The cause of your continued misfortune, therefore, has been that attitude of hauteur and undue pride. Go and seek his forgiveness and make him happy, and give my greetings to him.'

The merchant was greatly affected by this preknowledge. Moulana asked the merchant whether he would like to see the Frank Dervish at that very hour; and saying that, he (Moulana) touched the wall of his cloister, and thereby revealed a door, asking the merchant to look; and the merchant saw through that door the very crossroads as described by Moulana and saw the Dervish sleeping, as before.

The merchant in amazement tore his clothes like a madman and rode to the spot indicated by Moulana. When he arrived at the city in the western part of Frankistan (the land of the Franks), he sought the spot at the crossroads, and saw the Frank Dervish asleep there, as before. The merchant alighted from his mount at a fair distance in respect and solicitude and made obeisance towards the Frank Dervish. Seeing the merchant the Dervish said:

'I am powerless, otherwise I would have revealed to you, as also the power of God, had Moulana permitted me to reveal myself thus; but come near!' Saying this, the
* European

31

Dervish embraced the merchant with affection and kissed his beard; and added further, 'Now see my Master (Moulana).' And the merchant saw Moulana himself engaged in mystical audition, and uttering mysteries of mysticism and singing the verse: 'The ownership is His, whatever you have be happy — Be carnelian or become a ruby or only remain a clod of earth: If Fidelity thou seekest or Infidelity through desire (be that as it may). Tell thou to him "attach thyself to Truth" be thou a Frank'. Later when the merchant betook himself to the presence of Moulana, and conveyed the salutations of that Frank Dervish to Moulana, he (the merchant) gave as gifts many presents to the disciples of Moulana. Residing thereafter at Qonia, he became one of the devoted disciples of Moulana.

GLISTENING EYES

It is narrated that one night there was a great mystical audition function at the house of Moinuddin where a large number of learned persons and holy men were gathered; and Moulana was in mystical rapture and cried out repeatedly in ecstasy. After a while he went into a corner of the hall and stood there, and said after a moment that the reciters should stop awhile. All the sages who were present wondered at the request; meanwhile Moulana had plunged himself into a deep concentration; and then lifting his head, his two eyes ablaze with excitement looking like orbs of glistening blood; and said: 'Come friends behold in my eyes the grandeur of the Light of God!' Almost none dared to look at them; and whoever attempted it, his eyes dimmed and his sight became lacking immediately. The disciples raised a cry of mystical bliss.

Then Moulana looked at Chalabi Hisamuddin and said to him: 'Come, my object of troth and confidence; come forward, my most beloved, king of mine; the real king of mine, come forward to me!' Chalabi shrieked with excitement (at the praise conferred upon him) and tears ran down his cheeks. Maybe someone reporting the matter to Emir Tajuddin objected whether the great and distinguished qualities spoken about Hisamuddin were really meant, or was Moulana merely being polite to him. While this was being discussed Hisamuddin Chalabi arrived at the scene, he caught hold of the informant, and addressing himself to Moinuddin said: 'Although previously the terms used by Moulana did not really apply to me; but as soon as he (Moulana) spoke those words, they became a part of me, and the Holy Quran has it (*sura Yasin*):

> 'His Command, when He intends anything is
> only to say to it, Be, so it is.

'The work of the words of Moulana (though they cannot be likened to God's words; yet metaphorically) are immediate and do not depend upon or require any explaining. The verse has it:

> 'It is held that always copper is transmuted into
> gold by the Philosopher's Stone — but this
> Philosopher's Stone has made copper itself
> into the Philosopher's Stone.'

It is, therefore, not beyond the grace of Moulana towards his friends and disciples that thus these qualities might arise in the texture of his disciples. Those who had doubted his wisdom, after this explanation hung their heads in shame; and, having been convinced of the truth, thanked Moulana. One other confounding attribute of Moulana was that no one could meet his stare, for the luminosity of his eyes was so great that whosoever met his gaze, his eyes were compelled to be cast down.

It is narrated also, that the Head of the Teachers of the Seminary, one named Moulana Shamsuddin Malti (May Allah bless his soul) who was one of the important disciples, reported that he was in the garden of the Sage Hisamuddin with others with Moulana, who having immersed his feet in the flowing stream was giving esoteric discourses to those assembled; especially he was extolling the great mystical powers of Moulana Shamsi Tabrizi.

One of the Teachers of the Seminary known as Badruddin Walid, having been impressed by what Moulana was saying about Moulana Shams Tabrizi, heaved a sigh, and said: 'Woe to me, woe to me.' Moulana, hearing that, asked 'Why these sighs, and signs of sadness, and what occasion was there to express such sentiments?' The man replied that he was grieved by the fact that he had not had the good fortune to have met Moulana of Tabriz and so did not gain further light from this illustrious 'torch of mysticism'! Moulana became silent for a time upon hearing the explanation and then said: 'Although you have not had an approach to Moulana Tabrizi, you have arrived at the gateway of one in whose every hair a hundred thousand Tabrizis are attached and yet wonder at Tabrizi's wafting of mighty waves of occult influences!' He recited: 'Shamsuddin, who captured our heart's kingdom; in him our life is immersed.' Everyone present was delighted with the allusion to the great sage who was not present (and yet was so much thought of) and then he read a few verses from his poem:

> 'Suddenly my lips uttered the name,
> Of the rose and the Rose Garden;
>   Then he came —
> And placed his hand upon
> My mouth; and said:
> "I am the king:
> I am the soul of the Garden.

O illustrious one;
If you like to be unto like to me.
Then ever remember me." '

It is said that for a full forty days Badruddin was indisposed due to this meeting, and after seeking forgiveness recovered from his illness; and became very attached to Moulana.

BOOKS AND THE
INNER MEANING WITHIN BOOKS

In a like manner, Sheikh Mahmud related that once Qazi Moulana Izzuddin, who was a minister of Sultan Kai-Khusro, built a mosque in Qonia and associated it with the name of Moulana; and being a man of great gifts and virtue, he asked Moulana one day: 'Whatever learning you have acquired, we too, have studied those very books; but what you have "received" from those and express it, is so much beyond us; and what could that mean?' Moulana replied: 'Yes, it is true, but we have *absorbed* something from one or two pages from the Book of Learning of Allah; which have so far reached you: and "it is from the Grace of God, He vouchsafes it to whosoever He desires". The verse has it:

'Wisdom that the Zohal Star (Saturn) gives;
Does not match our penetration;
    And Utarid (Mercury) and Zohal put together,
May also impart knowledge to man.
    But God has graced us with
    A quality of spirit;
And our beings are knit with
    The knowledge of Hope;
Thus the Learning of divine wisdom
    Our only course and hope.'

Thereupon the celebrated Qadi, overwhelmed, burst into tears.

THE MYSTIC DANCE

It is also narrated that, Qadi Izzuddin was against the dance and music, which induce mystical feelings in man. One day, Moulana, greatly moved by spiritual ecstasy, came out of the seminary at the high-moment of mystical music. He approached the Qadi and shouted to him and asked him to come to the gathering where God was being praised; and pushing him forward, brought him to the meeting of those who love the Lord, as was befitting his state of non-conformity to the mystical experience. Forthwith he tore his garments in a fit of ecstasy, and like others plunged into mystical song, and danced around and around and shoted in excitement; and ultimately became one of the best disciples of Moulana.

THE PATH

Likewise, it is narrated that the Qadi of Qonia, one Iziddin, the Qadi of Amasia, and the Qadi of Siwas, who were all men of great piety and learning, one day enquired from Moulana, as to what was his 'Path'; and Moulana replied: 'This is my "Path" and enlightenment will come to the follower;' — meaning that his method of mystical practices was the path for others to pursue and the followers would be enlightened by his guidance; this, really emphasizing the fact that Sufi Cult has no 'text books' and it is the Murshid, or Spiritual Guide, who leads his disciples to the occult destination. All these three personages became his disciples.

THE PARROT AND THE BALD MAN

Further it is reported that when the Qadi of Adana had a mosque built and associated the building with the name of Moulana, the Qadi asked Moulana to give an address after the opening prayer at the new mosque; for the opening ceremony of which he had distributed a lot of money as largesse. Moulana delivered a sermon, in which he spoke of a bird which was bald (and thereby deduced an object lesson for the people from the story metaphorically). At the conclusion the great saint Kamaluddin praised Moulana for the skill of the narrative, given as it was with such delicacy and inoffensiveness that its sting was not perceived by those men who were bald in the congregation; for both the Qadis were bald, and they were presiding at the gathering; and neither felt the slightest stigma.

A QUARREL

In a like manner it is narrated that one day Moulana when walking in a street heard two men engaged in fierce altercation, hurling vituperations at each other. Moulana heard one of them say to the other; 'If you use one foul word to me, I will reply with a thousand in return.' Moulana came forward and said to them: 'Come, my friend, hurl your wrath upon me; for if you cast a thousand vituperations at me, you will not hear a single one from me!' The two were thus put to shame, and became friends through this wise advice.

THE GRAMMARIAN
AND THE WELL

It is further narrated that, Moulana Shamsuddin Malti
(May Allah bless his soul) related that once a learned man
came to Moulana with his students ostensibly to pay their
salutations to the great divine, but also inwardly hoping to
test the knowledge of Moulana and ask some questions. The
students, of course, had always thought that all that is to be
known of learning was 'in the bosom' of their own teacher;
and wanted to test the depth of Moulana's attainments.

The visitors were with courtesy received by Moulana
(who had guessed their motives) and gave a discourse on
divers subjects; and then, as was his wont to make a point,
he started to relate a metaphorical story about two young
theologians: one a grammarian and the one only a
'follower' of the mystical path though versed in the usual
knowledge of religion. Both of them went for a walk, and
during the conversation the one who did not attach too
much importance to mere words pronounced a word with
a slightly unusual inflection. The grammarian objected,
saying that he being in possession of greater knowledge
(hence rather proud of his knowledge acquired from books
alone) could not allow the word to be used in that way.
They argued for a long time, neither noticing a dry well,

and the grammarian fell in. He asked the other man to rescue him. The man said that he would pull him out only if he dropped his objection; but the grammarian would not yield and insisted upon his superior knowledge. The other man just left the grammarian where he was and went on his way.

Relating this metaphorical tale, Moulana turned emphatically on the subject of self-pride and praise; and said, 'Unless one shuns this "insistence" upon self-loftiness, one will always remain in the well of darkness — (a darkness seen by others and not by him) — an uncontrolled Ego is like unto the dark well of that grammarian, and an unnecessary sense of self-importance is the outcome of that feeling.' Hearing and appreciating this tale of mystic meaning, all of the visitors were highly impressed and became disciples.

THE DERVISH AND THE CAMEL

It is also narrated that one day those assembled in the presence of Moulana were singing the praises of the governor of the country, one Moinuddin; by saying that during his governorship everyone was in physical comfort and wellbeing and that his generosity was great. Moulana replied that that was the fact and a hundredfold true; but that there was another aspect also to life (meaning that merely physical leadership was not enough, and a spiritual leadership had also its honoured place) and related a story. Once a group of pilgrims were travelling towards Mecca on a pilgrimage, when the camel of a Dervish, who was in the caravan with them, fell ill; and whatever they did to him the camel would not rise to his feet. (Apparently, the Dervish was only receiving a courtesy ride and had no luggage of his own) so that the others removing the load from the back of the sick camel distributed it to other camels, and left the Dervish alone (without a mount). Moulana emphasized the need of taking the Dervish with the caravan, and recited the verses:

'Take thou a Guide with thee
For without one
This path is perilous, —
I have named the guide
A Star of Good Fortune;
For Guide he is not
Through age; but
Because of his mystical knowledge.'

THE DONKEY

It is also narrated that, one day Moulana was giving a discourse in the Seminary and relating the inner meaning of many mysteries, when he asked whether the audience of students and his disciples understood why it is said in the Holy Quran: 'Of all cries the braying of a donkey is the worst.'

Moulana said: 'Most animals and creatures when they utter sounds, pray and sing the praises of God; such as the camel, the she-camel; the humming of the bees, the sound that a wasp might make, but the donkey brays for no such purpose. He lifts his voice on only two occasions: when he is hungry and when he has a desire for mating. Likewise is a man,' said Moulana, 'in whose heart the love of the Lord finds no place, He is in fact a lesser being than a donkey.'

And he recited the verse thus:

'Those whose passions are
Like the donkey's
Are less than it!

If thou knowest not
The Path;
Then do
The reverse of that which
The donkey wants.'

Later he related a story about a king who asked another ruler to send him the worst kind of food, the worst type of man and the lowest animal. The king's royal friend sent him some bad food, an Armenian slave, and a donkey. In his letter he quoted the Quranic verse saying that the worst sound is the braying of a donkey.

It is also related that one day Moulana and his friends were going towards the garden of Chalibi Hisamuddin, Moulana had his mount as a donkey. About his mount he observed that he was following the saintly practice of riding on a donkey, because several prophets rode on donkeys — such as Seth, Ezra and Jesus.

> *Verse:*　Ride on the bare back of a donkey,
> 　　　　　O Thou the wise —
> 　　　　　For on the bare backs on donkeys rode
> 　　　　　The Messengers of God.

At that time the saintly Shahabuddin was also riding on a donkey, and it began to bray. Angered by the sound, Shahabuddin started beating his mount on the head; whereupon Moulana admonished him, saying: 'Do not beat it; but thank God that you are riding and that the animal is not riding you.' Shahabuddin was ashamed, and as a recompense dismounted and kissed the hooves of the donkey. Further, Moulana observed: 'As many men are actuated by the same emotions, equitably it would be necessary to beat up most men.'

WORLDLY LOSS

Also it is narrated that one day a man came to Moulana and complained bitterly about his worldly losses, and how poverty dogged his footsteps. Moulana counselled him to shun his company, and added, 'Do not come near us, and keep away from us and the people like us, so that worldly fortune might come near you,' and recited:

'Come and be like me,
O thou noble one;
And seek neither the
Heights nor the depths of
Perishable things:
For if the Devil's texture were made in
That way —
Then he would have been bedecked
With a kingly crown,
And draped in the sages' garb.'

It is likewise narrated that once the Prophet Mohammed said to one of those who were present 'Wear iron gloves and welcome adversities and be prepared to undergo hardships; because the frown of worldly fortune is as a gift to those who love their Lord.'

Moulana related that once a mystic asked a wealthy man which did he love more, Sin or Money. The man replied that he loved money more. The mystic said: 'You do not tell the truth, for you will leave your riches behind and will take your deeds with you.'

'Do something,' continued the mystic, 'that you take that which you love most (money) with you: (that is by spending in good causes and in charity) and so that you might send your riches to God before your arrival before God: for it is in the Quran. "And whatever of good you send on beforehand for yourselves, you will find it with God; that is the best and greatest reward." '

THE PLACE OF HONOUR

It is further narrated that, one day many close friends and men of piety and learning were invited by the saintly Moinuddin to his residence; and had already sat themselves at the places of honour as befitted their status in learning. But the High Governor wished that Moulana should also grace the occasion. Mujadadeen the son-in-law of the Governor, was sent to fetch Moulana. Meantime, among the gathering of distinction appeared a sense of embarrass-ment about where the Moulana would sit, since every seat of honour was taken. Everyone, content with his own sense of dignity, resolved that when Moulana arrived, he would just sit in whatever place was available. (None of them was going to offer his seat of honour, all being important persons themselves). The one who was sent to fetch Moulana used fitting words of invitation. Moulana, taking the saintly Chalibi Hisamuddin and other friends, started towards the house.

The followers of Moulana walked ahead. As soon as the saintly Hisamuddin stepped into the house, all the great sages made places of honour available for him. Later Moulana arrived and the Governor hurried to receive him and kissed his hand as a token of respect. Seeing that all the great dignitaries were already in occupation of seats of honour, he merely saluted them and sat down in the space beyond the chief platform.

The saintly Chalibi Hisamuddin, seeing Moulana sitting in the space beyond, left his place and sat beside Moulana. Noting that other men of importance, too, came to where Moulana was sitting (but those who grudged to acknowledge the greatness of Moulana continued to sit in their high places) such as Sheikh Nasiruddin and Sayed Sharifuddin and men like him; each in his turn was learned in his own right, as if he had studied a whole library of books. They say that Sharifuddin was a man of high qualities and of knowledge, and yet somewhat outspoken and a little forward in speech. Therefore, seeing that Moulana had attracted most to his side from the row of honour, where seats were now empty, he asked where was the place of the chief guest and who really was to be considered president of the gathering.

Sheikh Sharifuddin voiced the opinion that according to the saints of Khurasan, and those who have the cloistered life, the place of honour was the angle of the platform. But Sheikh Sadruddin said that the most honourable place was at the far end of the dais in the realm of the Sufis; and then as a test they asked Moulana to state the place of honour. The Moulana recited:

> 'Is there any meaning
> In the terms or the habitation and
> Who presides?
>
> Who are we and I —
> We are where the Beloved is.'

'The President is where the Beloved is' said Moulana; and Sayed Sharifuddin asked: 'Where is the Beloved?' 'O thou blind one, seest thou not?' said Moulana and recited the verse:

> 'You have no inward eyes to see —
> Otherwise;
> You would perceive
> In your whole being —
> From top to toe,
> Is no art, but His.'

Later when Moulana departed from this world, and Sharifuddin arrived at Damascus, he had lost his sight (a prediction of Moulana); and then he used to weep and cry. He said that when Moulana shouted at him, he felt that they held a large black tray before his eyes, with the consequence that he could neither determine the colour of things, nor see anything clearly. But he hoped that Moulana, whose sense of forgiveness was limitless, would forgive him for his arrogance; and recited the verse saying:

> 'Do not lose hope of
> Forgiveness
> The sea of remission is vast,
> If thou recant.
> For thy sins ask for forgiveness,
> In prayer and meditation:
> For His forgiveness is beyond measure.'

It is also narrated that, this incident took place at the house of Jalaluddin Qaratai. Having had his seminary completed, he invited a large number of learned men and men of importance on the occasion of the opening ceremony of the College, the Madrasa.

On that day Moulana Shamsi Tabriz had newly arrived in the town; and sitting on the platform amongst other men of learning, asked Moulana which was the seat of honour at a gathering. Moulana replied, 'The seat of honour among men of learning is in the centre of the platform; and the place of honour of the "men seeking the mysteries of mysticism" is in the corner; and the place of honour of the Sufis at the end of the platform; and the place of honour of those who love is beside the loved one'. And saying this, he left his place and sat beside Moulana Shams; and it is related that Moulana Shamsi Tabrizi became better known to the people of Qonia after that.

It is narrated, too, that once the governor Moinuddin had invited people to a mystical musical gathering in honour of Moulana. Many men of saintly pursuits and mystical thought were present. The atmosphere rose to great heights until midnight; with the consequence that all the food became cold and uneatable. The servant of the host whispered this in the ear of his master; who sought an opportunity to mention the fact to Moulana in a suitable manner. (Moulana sensed the meaning). And observed: 'How can a man standing beside a water-mill stop the motion of the mill, when waters pour down with force uncontrollable?'

The host wept in emotion on hearing this allegory. The food was distributed to the poor; and fresh food was prepared.

MIRACLE OF THE MEDICAMENTS

It is also narrated that once the greatest of all contemporary physicians of Roum prepared medicine and pills to cure seventy persons that might be bitten by snakes. This was done in accordance with the commands of the then king; who, likewise, ordered that seventy cups of purgative drugs should also be got ready for eventualities.

It so happened, however, that when these drugs were ready and prepared, Moulana visited the physician's residence. As was customary, Moulana was received with due honour by the noted physician, Akmaluddin by name. Moulana, noticing the seventy-odd cups of medicine, drank one cup after another; and after each drastic draught, he (Moulana) thanked God for the excellence of the taste thereof.

The medical man was so stunned that he could hardly speak, nor dared he inform Moulana about the energetic effect of that medicine upon a normal person. Having gulped down these potent drugs, Moulana walked away unconcernedly to his seminary; and the disciples were informed by the doctor about it. They, like him, were very anxious as to the result of the medicine upon the health of their Master; a Master, who, in the nature of things had to be very careful of his wellbeing for he had undergone severe physical strain during his long life of prayer and exercises, and might not be able to stand up to a single dose. The physician could not rest contented. In great anxiety of mind, he betook himself to the place where Moulana lived. He found Moulana sitting in the archway, immersed in a book of inner philosophy, and serenely reading the text.

After dutiful salutations, the physician delicately enquired how Moulana felt. He was told that Moulana was as cool and happy as if he were beside cooling rivers. The physician delicately suggested that it might be wise to desist from drinking cool water; whereupon Moulana ordered iced water to be brought. He put some ice in it, further, to chill it, and started sucking little bits of ice and he drank that water to the full. Then he went to the bath, after which he commanded that mystical music should be played; and continued to listen to the chanting for three days without interruption.

The physician clamoured that such a manifestation of disregard for medical potency was beyond all human experience, and this could only be done by saints: thereupon he, with all his sons and family and those related to him became disciples of Moulana; and he related the experience to his fellow physicians.

The verse has it:

> If he drinks poison, it becomes inert for him —
> But, if the 'unripe seeker' drinks it
> He might, due to the venom, become
> As blue as blue mice!

It is this that made no effect
Upon the Great First Caliph — Abu Bakr —
For to him, poison worked as sugar.

The allusion is to the incident,when The First Caliph
Abu Bakr, accompanying The Prophet Mohammed on his
Flight from Mecca to Medina was hiding from their
enemies in a cave and a snake projected its head from a hole
in the cave; and Abu Bakr put his big toe on the hole, and
the snake struck, but the poison did not do him any harm.

MIRACLE OF THE BLOOD

Likewise, it is narrated that, during that time a great intellectual controversy arose amongst the physicians, whether man was linked by virtue of the blood in his veins, or through the Mercy of God alone. The doctors of medicine naturally held the opinion that as blood was the life-sap of a human body, if it was drained out, life would terminate.

The thinkers of the esoteric type held a different view. They posed the question to Moulana.

He said that in medicine, quite naturally, the existence of blood in the human body is essential: 'But in our way of thinking man's existence is bound up with the Will of God, and none can or should gainsay that.' So saying, he called for a man to blood-let him. He had himself bled to the extent that normal men would have expired and so much blood was removed that the body showed a yellowish colour, being practically drained of all blood. He drew this to the attention of the physicians, and asked whether they did not believe that man lives through the Mercy of God, and not by blood alone.

They all bowed their heads in agreement and became his disciples; then he went to his bath; and was thereafter joined in the chanting and singing of mystical verses, as if nothing unusual had occurred.

WHY SAGES SPEAK OF SAINTS

It is also narrated that once Moulana Shamsuddin Malti visited the residence of Moulana, and found him sitting alone. The Master asked him to come and sit closer to him. Thereupon Malti sat closer; but Moulana asked him closer still; and yet closer, until Malti's knees touched those of the Moulana; and then the Moulana spoke about the great attainments of Sayed Burhanuddin and Moulana Shamsi Tabrizi, until Malti became overwhelmed with it all; thereupon Moulana, by way of explanation, said:

'You so feel, because where anyone talks about the sublimity of pious people, there the benignity of God falls like a gracious rain; and refreshes the mind.'

It is also narrated that whenever Moulana used to go to the bath, and his wife had given the disciples a silk mat, so that after a hot bath he might not get a chill.

One day when they were unfolding the silken quilt for the purpose, Moulana (seeing all this, and noting the reason of it), at once shed the garments which were protecting him from the cold weather, and stepped out into the severe cold of the yard outside. The disciples saw that instead of wrapping himself up with warm clothing, he was standing on the snow-covered yard. He had placed a large piece of ice upon his head. By way of explanation he said to his disciples:

IMPERVIOUS TO COLD

'O, my friends do not let my material-self be pampered; I am not from the clan of the Pharoahs; but of the tribe of that king who was the king of the great Dervishes.' Saying that, he put on his hat and walked away.

THE UNRULY SELF

Likewise it is narrated that Hadrat Sultan Walad (the son of Moulana) said that when Moulana was as young as the age of five years, his desires and cravings had already died out. 'My father attained his majority, and then his years reached middle age. He was constantly subjecting himself to the rigours of prayer. In a sense of self-abnegation, he disregarded all material comforts and suppressed his desires for worldly things. I asked him why, when his desires were suppressed at that early age, did he persist in renunciation, still as watchful as ever about physical wants and desires? He replied that the Self is a great trickster, and 'one has always to be alert in case that evil overpowers one.'

> Pull the bridle of the Unruly Self,
> Ever hard —
> Beware of the snares of the world's
> Faithless flowers;
> Believing not in his holy garb,
> Or his long string of prayer-beads,
> Neither allying oneself with him;
> Nor jointly riding hard with him.

ADMISSION OF A DISCIPLE

It is also related that Chalibi Hisamuddin reported that Sayed Sharifuddin had a great friend, a notable man in Qonia; who had a son of grace and intelligence. The young man was greatly impressed by Moulana's piety and goodness, and desired to become a disciple, even at an early age. The youth's father, thinking that Moulana's teachings were too advanced for the lad, reserved his permission. But the young man threatened to commit suicide unless he was given permission to become a devotee of the great sage. The boy's father ultimately consented and approached Sayed Sharifuddin about the matter. Sharifuddin, rather than give a negative reply to the father, laid a plan. He suggested that the father should ask Moulana whether his son would go to paradise or not. An insolent question might anger Moulana, and permission to enrol him as one of the disciples might be withheld.

The father of the young man gave a great feast for the learned of the town. After this, as was usual, a mystical dance and musical concert was held. When the manifestations and performance were at their height, the father asked the suggested question. Without hesitation, Moulana replied that the young man was destined to go to paradise, and was fit to behold the grace of God. He was not like others of his age in the town; because he was attracted by spiritual teachings, and they were not. Thereupon the father of the young man, as well as the son, became disciples of Moulana.

POOR QUALITY OF DISCIPLES

It is also narrated that one day Moinuddin, the celebrated, observed the 'Moulana was a man of great piety, and like unto him none had been born for generations'; but that his disciples were of poor quality and self-seekers.

One of those present on the occasion reported the conversation to Moulana, and his disciples were greatly grieved.

Moulana thereupon sent a note to the man who had made the observation; saying that if his disciples were already men of quality, he would have become their disciple and not they his; because they were lacking in virtue he accepted them in order to 'refine' them. He then said: 'I swear by the soul of my honoured father, that till God became the grace-protector of those men so that such men might tread the right path of acceptance, they were not enrolled as my disciples.' He recited:

> 'Strayed they are,
> Lingering they were
> In the Path of Godly Things:
> To their rescue, we have come;
> To the aid of such, we have to strive.'

When Moinuddin received the letter of Moulana, he was so moved by the argument that he immediately became his follower and served him faithfully ever after.

TELEPATHIC VISIT

It is also narrated that near Moulana's Seminary lived a young merchant, who was attracted by the teachings. This youth, however, was very anxious to travel to Egypt, although his friends advised against it. When Moulana heard of the plan he, too, pronounced against the journey. The merchant, however, was determined to travel. One fine night he started towards Syria. Reaching Antakia, he boarded a ship bound for Egypt. As ill-luck would have it, the ship was captured by the Franks and with it the young merchant, who was flung into a dungeon. He was very poorly fed. For fully forty days he remained in that dark cell, and constantly wailed that this imprisonment was due to his disobeying his spiritual master — Moulana.

On the fortieth night, however, he saw Moulana in a dream, who said that the next morning, when he (the merchant) was to be interrogated by his Frank captors, to every question put to him he was to reply in the affirmative. He woke with a start, and sure enough, when the Franks came to question him with a translator: asking whether he knew anything about medicine, he — as instructed in his dream the previous night — said that he was an expert medical man. The Franks were very pleased to hear that, and asked him to come immediately to see their king, who was ill and needed urgent medical attention.

The prisoner was given suitable clothes, and taken to the palace at once, as a 'distinguished physician'. On the way an inspiration came to him; and, after seeing the patient, he prescribed that seven kinds of fruits were to be brought and their juice extracted, and given to the patient. By the Grace of God the king's ailment took an immediate turn for the better. The king was greatly pleased and the young merchant thenceforward became an honoured guest. Even although that young man was completely illiterate, yet help came to him:

> Sublime hearts come to aid
> When the cry of the oppressed
> Reaches them, for help.

When the king regained his normal health, he asked the merchant in what way he could reward him. The young merchant asked merely to be released and sent home in order to bend his knee before his spiritual master. He was released and gifts were given to him; and he now related his story to the Franks, who were considerably impressed by Moulana's help and spiritual powers.

When the merchant reached Qonia, he went straight to Moulana's house. Kissing his feet, he touched them in thanksgiving and reverence. Moulana expressed his pleasure at seeing the young merchant, and kissed his disciple's face affectionately, remarking: 'After this experience of pleasing the Franks, and securing your release, now endeavour even more than before to earn a living in contentment and in righteousness; for contentment is a mercy of God, and greed leads to the darkness of dungeons.'

RICH AND POOR

It is likewise narrated that one day some zealous disciples of Moulana expressed regret that the more important people of the town did not visit Moulana, but often went to much lesser men of learning and piety. They considered that those citizens did not fully appreciate the greatness of Moulana. To all this, Moulana replied that, if he received the wealthy and important men of the town, then the poorer would be deprived of his company.

It was as if the complaint of the disciples of Moulana 'travelled to the ears' of the richer community of Qonia. The very next morning a large number of those endowed with worldly substance in the city arrived to be blessed by Moulana. Amongst them were such men of standing as Fakhruddin, Moinuddin, Halaluddin Mustafa, and Aminuddin Miakayal. The terrace of Moulana's house was filled to overflowing with the celebrities of the city, and there was no room left in the seminary for the poorer disciples to listen to the discourse of their Master.

In consequence such people had to stand outside the house, receiving little or no attention from Moulana — a matter of great unhappiness to those less fortunate in worldly goods. As soon, however, as the rich gentry left the terrace, the poor disciples came in and complained respectfully to Moulana at having been left out. The Master pacified them by saying that his real friends were the poor; and that his preaching and discourses were always dedicated to the humbler and less rich, and that the rich in effect received the instructions as 'a residue' of those of the poor; as for instance people drink the milk of goats *after* their young have been supplied with milk by their mothers. The residue is for the wealthier, and the fuller virtue was fed to the poorer disciples. Moulana further added that the influx occurred because the poorer disciples themselves had complained in the first place about the non-attendance of the gentry. Moulana had not invited them himself. The disciples, therefore, should not take it ill, and should pray that the richer class might always tread the right path of virtue and not trouble the Dervishes, but continue to earn their livelihood in peace and contentment.

THE NAME OF A CITY

It is also narrated that, one day Moulana had been attending a meeting at a house where Sheikh Ziauddin was reciting the Quranic text in which the following verse occurred:

> Consider the early hours of
> the Dawn,
> And the night when it
> Covers with darkness.
> Your Lord has not forsaken you,
> Nor has He become displeased (with you).*

This verse affected Moulana greatly; but Hisamuddin apologised that the reciter did not recite the Quran in simple tones, but rather with an affectation.

Moulana observed that this reminded him of an incident when a grammarian, who was on a journey asked a simple Seeker whether that was the town which he had been seeking. The grammarian's high-faluting pronunciation did not quite conform to the simple usage of the locality; and, therefore, the unassuming Seeker simply replied that he had never heard the name of such a city.

* *Sura* 93, 1-3, *'The Glorious Morning Light'*.

This meant, of course, that although the text of the Quran was the same as that which Moulana knew, yet by the affectation of the reciter it lacked the simplicity of the spirit.

The grammarian in the story insisted that the proper pronunciation was just what he was using; and the Seeker replied that that might well be the case, but the citizens of that city spoke the name in a certain way, and so the grammarian must mean another city.

THE LADDER AND THE ROPE

It is also narrated that once Moulána was giving a discourse on the higher aspects of spiritual philosophy. He included in his narration a story that a Dervish was passing a dry well in which a grammarian had fallen by accident on a dark night; and the unfortunate man cried out for help. The Dervish called out to other men to fetch a rope and a ladder to rescue the man in the well. But the grammarian shouted up to the Dervish that according to proper usage, he ought to employ the word 'ladder' first and the word 'rope' afterwards. Thereupon the Dervish replied: 'Remain where you are till I learn proper diction!'

Moulana deduced the lesson from this story that those who are constantly engaged in hair-splitting and do not try to reveal the inner meanings of things are like the man in the well. They remain in the difficulties of their self-assumed scholarship; nor do they seek a master who might lead them to the worthwhile spiritual destination.

It is likewise narrated that the saintly Salahuddin had a disciple, who was very much attached to Moulana, and was in the business of buying and selling. This merchant was for long nursing the thought of visiting Istanbul. When he had made all the arrangements, he came to say goodbye to Moulana and to seek his blessing and grace.

THE MONK AND THE MIRACLE

Moulana said to the merchant that when he was in Istanbul he should visit a Christian monk, who had renounced the world, and lived in the neighbourhood; and should convey to him Moulana's greetings and salutations. Upon arriving in the city of the Turks, the very first thing that the merchant did was to visit the Frankish monk whom he found in profound contemplation with a halo of righteousness around him. With much respect, the merchant conveyed the greetings of Moulana to the monk, and the monk rose with respect to receive those expressions of friendship. Then the monk bent his knees in prayer.

The merchant could not help glancing around the cloister. To his bewilderment, he saw Moulana sitting in a corner, also in deep contemplation. Moulana wore the same clothes, the same turban and the same expression on his face as he had seen when he had bade him goodbye at Qonia. The merchant was so shocked by this manifestation that he became unconscious. When he recovered, the monk pacified him. He said if he (the merchant) could become aware of the mysteries of the 'free' he would become higher in spiritual level. The monk gave him a letter to those responsible to afford all facilities to the merchant in his travels and work.

The merchant brought that letter to the king at Istanbul, who gave him a royal welcome and fulfilled all his requirements. After that he went back to the monk to take leave of that man of piety; and the monk, like Moulana, commissioned the merchant to carry his greetings to Moulana and to say that Moulana might graciously not forget to send his blessings to the monk. When, however, the merchant returned to his home in Qonia, he related the incidents of his journey to the Sheikh Salahuddin, who observed that whatever saintly persons say is ever correct, but advised the merchant not to recite the facts of this mystical happening to those who did not belong to the esoteric 'fold'. Thereupon he took the merchant to Moulana to whom he conveyed the salutations of the Christian monk in Istanbul. Moulana said to the merchant:

'Look, and you will see wonder!' What did the merchant then behold to his utter wonderment but that the monk sat in the corner of Moulana's room in deep contemplation and wore the same garments as the merchant had seen him wear in Istanbul!

The merchant tore his clothes in the ecstasy of the whole scene; for the thing had passed all human comprehension. Moulana took the merchant aside and said: 'After what you have seen, you have seen hidden mysteries, and you are now our confidant; do not reveal these facts to the unworthy, those of little knowledge of mystic lore.' And then Moulana recited a couplet:

'The one who may not
reveal the secret of the Sultan —
Nor cast sugar before the ants.

He alone can receive the secrets;
Otherwise, it is like throwing jewels
before the cows.'

The merchant was greatly moved, gave all his fortune to the poor, and, renouncing worldly affairs, became a devoted disciple of the Master.

It is also narrated that, one day Moulana was going towards the town from his mosque, when he saw a bearded monk; and asked him whether his white beard was older than his age. To this the monk replied that he had grown his beard since he was twenty years of age.

'Then you are older than your beard' observed Moulana. He continued, 'it is a great pity that that which is younger than you has become white with virtue and holiness, and you remain the same in the dark alleys of life, and you continue in the path which your beard has not taken.'

The monk at once saw the point, broke his rosary; and, joining the faith, became one of the great disciples of Moulana.

In like manner, once they saw a group of those with black robes; and the disciples pitied them for having strayed from the true path, and as people who had no real thought of spiritual life and mystic feeling. The disciples reflected that if the sun of guidance could shine upon the blackness of those berobed persons, even quite by accident, they could have their path enlightened. As soon as these men came within sight of Moulana — 'the sun shone upon them' — and they immediately came to the path trod by Moulana and ultimately became devoted disciples. It is said that God conceals darkness in whiteness, and produces whiteness from darkness. Hearing this wise saying, the disciples bent their heads further in acceptance of the truths uttered by Moulana.

PERFECTING THE INNER BEING

It is likewise narrated that once Moulana Ikhtiaruddin Faqih, the famous Doctor of Law, was late in returning from the Friday prayer to the house of Moulana, despite the fact that Moulana had asked for his presence several times. Upon his return Moulana asked him the cause of his delay. The Doctor replied that he was detained because a preacher from Khojand was delivering a sermon — during which it was difficult for him to leave the congregation. Moulana asked what was the text upon which the preacher's discourse was based; and he was informed that the Mullah of Khojand spoke on the point of the good fortune that he and his audience enjoyed in being what they were; and exhorted upon his hearers to give thanks to God that he and they were not born outside the fold of the Faith. Moulana said with a smile: 'The poor Mullah has exalted himself over the prophets and saints in saying that and feeling that they were the only exalted ones. Such men do not perceive their inward self — (meaning that these people were great sinners and had little insight into their mystical being, and they looked only upon the "outer" self of the human being, neglecting the mystery of mystic meaning), and these people do not realise the excellence of those who had perfected their "inner-being" with "mystic light".' And then Moulana recited a poem:

> 'There are those,
> Whose wings beat
> Around the Throne of Allah;
> And the angels and saintly men
> Are those who love the Lord.'

STONE INTO RUBY

It is also narrated that the great littérateur Hisamul-Millah-wa-Din Amasi, who in addition to his other qualities was also one of the major disciples, related that one Badruddin Tabrizi, who was skilled in mathematics, astronomy, chemistry and history, had related amongst the friends that he was one of those who had taken part with Moulana at a mystical music-meeting until dawn one night in the garden of Chalabi Hisamuddin; and at dawn Moulana allowed the disciples to close their eyes in sleep for a short while; whilst he himself plunged himself into deep contemplation; and Badruddin said: 'I, too, reclined to rest, but my mind was at work; for I was thinking that great persons, like Seth, and Jesus, and Idris, and Solomon, and Luqman and Khizr — all of great mystical attainments — had manifested miracles — and these men of high qualities had extraordinary mastery and dexterity; for instance in curing skins, high crafts of transmuting baser metals into gold and the like, which were beyond all human capabilities; and I wondered as to whether Moulana was blessed with any of such qualities.

'I was in such thoughts, when suddenly, as if a tiger had jumped at me Moulana called hoarsely my name, and placed a piece of stone in my left hand, and said: "Go and give thanks to God"; and when I looked closely at the stone, it had turned into a giant ruby of such quality that I had not seen in the treasury of any king. This incident so affected me that I cried out and those of my compatriots who were sleeping woke up and asked me why I shouted and at such an hour, yelling like the voices of ten persons.'

Badruddin added that he wept a long time, seeking the forgiveness of Moulana, for thinking thuswise about what supernatural phenomena he could perform. Moulana forgave him, and then he took the 'converted stone — ruby' to Moulana's daughter and gave it to her as a gift. She at once converted the ruby into money: one hundred and eight thousands dirhams — and spent the sum upon the various necessities of the disciples and needy men and women.

Moulana, commenting upon the incident later, enquired whether we had not heard the story of a Dervish who had changed the dry branch of a tree into a bow of solid gold, and that type of people were his friends; and further added that although it was a matter of great wonderment to convert lifeless objects (stones and vegetables) into precious metals; yet it was a greater quality to convert the soul and mind of the living into mystical 'gold'; and he recited:

> 'Of a truth wonderful it is,
> To transmute copper into gold
> By the Philosopher's Stone!
> But note the wonder still, that
> A 'copper' converts minute after minute
> The Philosopher's Stone!'

SHOES OF IRON

It is also narrated that Moulana Shamsuddin Malti (May Allah bless his soul) related that when Sheikh Mazharuddin son of Sheikh Saifuddin Bakharzi (Allah bless his soul) reached Qonia, a large number of the learned people and others of status came to meet him; and gave him much respect and attention due to his sanctity and piety. Quite by accident, it so happened that on that day Moulana was passing the Sheikh's resthouse with his disciples; and Sheikh Mazharuddin perhaps might have said that the news of the arrival of the great sage had not reached the ears of Moulana — indirectly suggesting that Moulana was expected to come to see the visitor.

One of the disciples, hearing the suggestion, mentioned the matter to Moulana, who observed that the man who was the real 'visitor' was he and not the man who had come to Qonia; and thus it was more true that the Sheikh should have come first to see him and not he to go to the Sheikh. The disciples were, however, unable to follow the comment and sought an explanation, and were told in the following terms: 'We have arrived here from the city of Baghdad of That Who is All in All which pervades all that is. And that brother of ours had only come from a street of the "mere" Baghdad (of stone and clay); thus we are the real "visitors" and not he.' The allusion here is a mystical one, meaning that men soaked in the mystery of mysticism see God in everything, every stone, and leaf; and appreciate the 'oneness of God' in the 'oneness' of all that exists. When the report reached the visiting Sheikh he, too, being a 'man of virtue and inward appreciation' acknowledged the true meaning, and came to pay his respects to Moulana, and became one of his great devotees. And the visiting sage further added that whatever his father had said was true: that one ought to wear shoes of iron (that do not get broken by long walks) and to have a staff of iron for rest, and to go in search of a master like the Moulana for spiritual uplift.

IF GOD WILLS...

It is also narrated that, one day Moulana asked his servant, one Sheikh Mohammed, to perform a certain task; to which the servant replied 'Yes, *Inshaallah*.' (Yes, if God Wills). At once Moulana yelled, 'You fool! Who but God's manifestation orders you to do this task?' Here the allusion is not that Moulana claimed to be divine: but that, according to the mystical idea, God's attributes are so closely identified with man's actions and he is so much under the governance of God's will and purpose that the man is nothing but an instrument of His manifestation, being the 'best of the creation' and that Oneness of all things that exist make the Infinite as One with all that was, is and will be. The servant was overwhelmed with the force of the spiritual command, and asked to be forgiven.

MYSTICAL RAPTURE

It is likewise narrated that one day Moinuddin had invited a number of notables, and the Sultan also was present; the major guest being Moulana. The mystical audition lasted until well past midnight; and perhaps one of the disciples had whispered to the host that if the audition was terminated the people might snatch some sleep. Without knowing what was said, Moulana asked for the sound to cease; but whilst others began to rest, one named Shiekh Abdur-Rahman Sayyad still was shouting loudly in a kind of ecstasy. The Sultan whispered to one that Abdur-Rahman was showing strange manners; that although all had been resting, or trying to sleep, Abdur-Rahman still continued to yell and shout; 'And', said the Sultan, 'Is that Dervish a greater person to be moved with the occasion than Moulana, who was silent and reposeful?' To which Moulana observed that in the heart of some were earthly desires like monstrous dragons; which would not allow them to rest or come forward like other disciples, to gain mystical refinement; for the dragon continued to pull them aside. The Sultan was so impressed that he begged to be admitted into the ranks of the disciples.

CALLING UPON MOULANA

It is also narrated that the reason of the eventual dismantling of the House of the Seljuks was this, that the Sultan had become a humble disciple of Moulana and had considered Moulana his spiritual father. But slowly his allegiance became suspect, for he had been made to pay much greater attention to one who was a mere 'showman' in matters of mystical performance. A group of men of much less religious importance had praised this man so highly that the Sultan inclined towards him more and more.

One day, however, a breaking point arrived, for the Sultan invited a number of highly-placed men, including Moulana and pronounced that he (the Sultan) had thenceforward accepted the spiritual guidance of the other man — name as Sheikh Baba Marvizi — in preference to Moulana, and that from that date onward Marvizi was his spiritual father.

A public affront of this kind quite naturally affected Moulana, who said that if the Sultan had taken another as his spiritual father, then he, too, would seek another spiritual son; and left the gathering. It is also narrated that Chalabi Hisamuddin reported that as he left the Sultan's gathering along with Moulana, he experienced a 'vision' that the Sultan was standing without his head, as if the Sultan's head were cut off; and although many men of learning ran after the enraged Moulana, he did not return to the King's meeting. After a few days, the Sultan invited the more important divines to perform an incense-burning ceremony so that the danger of the Mongol invasion might be averted.

After this ceremony the King came to seek the blessing of Moulana, for he was then going to face the Mongols. Moulana advised that the King should not go, but as the news of the danger was insistent, he had no option but to go and face the enemy, but before he launched out far he met his fate. When he reached Aq Sarai and was putting on his bow and arrow case, they strangled him, and he is said to have called for help from Moulana. It so happened that at that hour Moulana was in an ecstasy of mystic songs, and during the performance asked a lute to be brought to him with which he plugged his ear; another was placed on the other ear of Moulana, and then he could hear nothing, it is said. A little later, he placed his wrap in the archway and invited his disciples to perform with him the prayers for the dead. At the conclusion of all this, the disciples wished to be enlightened as to why their Master had plugged his ears, and had performed the rites for the dead; and he replied: 'I had made my ears soundproof, because I heard the cry of the King (though the scene was many miles away) who was beseeching me for my help; and I could not help, because it was but the will of God that he should die' (this was the same Sultan who had taken another man as his spiritual 'father' despite the fact that he had been previously accepted as the spiritual son by Moulana, and he had publicly affronted the Master) 'and the prayer was for the soul of the man'.

THE MYSTERIOUS FLIGHT

It is also narrated that some time prior to this happening at a mystical audition-meeting Moulana sat with the disciples from early forenoon to late at night. Towards the conclusion of this meeting the saintly Chalabi Hisamuddin felt very sleepy. Noticing this Moulana spread his mantle for him to recline upon, and Chalabi dropped off to sleep. During this sleep he dreamt that a large white bird came and took him in its talons and flew to regions far above the earth, so high that the earth appeared as a small speck. In that region the bird descended on the top of a mountain, a mountain as fertile and full of vegetation as if God had created it from a large piece of green jewel. On the top of that mountain Chalabi saw a head like a human head; and thereupon the bird gave a sword into the hand of Chalabi saying that he should cut the throat of that head, which, added the bird, was the command of God. Chalabi asked the bird who he was and received the reply that the bird was a companion of Gabriel. Chalabi having performed the action asked for, was lifted by the bird and deposited on the very spot on earth from which he had flown upwards. When Chalabi awoke, he saw Moulana standing beside him.

PART OF A GREATER WHOLE

It is also narrated that once Sheikh Mahmud Najjar the Saintly related that on an occasion Moulana was giving a discourse on matters of the high philosophy of mystic thought, when the great sage Shamsuddin arrived on the scene; and Moulana welcomed him by saying: 'He (the sage) often speaks about God and His manifestations; and now on this occasion he (the sage) will hear of God directly (through one inspired) and,' said Moulana, 'a day will come when God's words will be known directly without a Sheikh as an interpreter . . . because the Real Sheikh is He alone; and He is He and the Sheikh are one; and the Oneness means that the disciples and the Sheikhs are all part of a greater Whole; and That and This and He and Who are but words and mere illusions;' and he recited the following couplet:

> 'He, The Greatest of All Kings;
> Men thought, was behind the doors
> In the Locked House of Existence;
> But donning the robes of a Dervish
> A voice can convey the meaning of
> The Greatest of All.'

It is also narrated that, Sheikh Mahmud related that one day there was a meeting of mystical audition in the seminary of Sheikh Sadruddin, and Moulana attended the meeting; and the sound swelled to an extraordinary degree, lifting the atmosphere of feeling to high levels. Kamaluddin suggested that with all the greatness of Moulana, his disciples did not include men of high status, but were either carpenters, or tailors or craftsmen of humbler origin. When the remark was conveyed to Moulana, he called loudly to Kamaluddin, and said 'If that be so, Mansoor was not a man of great public importance from the wealth point of view, nor was Sheikh Abu Bakr (not the Caliph) who was but a carpenter; and yet after the name of these men you say "blessed be their names"; and that was because they were men of great mystical attainments. In what way did their humbler callings detract from their spiritual attainments?' The one who had made the comment felt very ashamed of himself, and asked for forgiveness.

SHOCKS

It is likewise narrated that on one occasion a man named Kamal (meaning 'perfection') in a meeting turned his back towards the humbler disciples of Moulana; and took little notice of them. Moulana did not like it; and shouted: 'O, you Bay-Kamal' (*Bay* makes a negative of Kamal: that is, without excellence — a play upon words) and the voice of Moulana terrified him to the extent that he, Kamaluddin, fell to the stone floor and grievously hurt his head and asked for forgiveness. Moulana forgave the man and bestowed upon him his cloak and a turban, and he became a devout disciple.

HUMILITY

It is likewise narrated that one of the discourses of Moulana emphasized the virtue and necessity of humbleness of bearing in life. He said that trees which shoot up in the air and pride themselves only on their height, may have no fruits; but those which give fruit have their boughs weighed down with the fruit and the nobility thereof. It was for that reason that the Prophet Mohammed (Peace be upon him) was polite and humble to a high degree; and thus excelled other prophets in this respect and in being a true Dervish; and he said 'Always deal with people with courtesy and humbleness, and see that none is hurt by you (materially or mentally);' and, therefore, when during an attack which enemies made upon him they broke one of the Prophet's teeth, he only prayed to God to direct his people towards the right path for he added, 'They do not know the right path'; and, of course (in place of cursing them or praying to have the wrath of God to be brought down upon them) he loved them and only asked not for their destruction but for their being guided to the right path, and he himself forgave them. It is said, therefore, that before the Prophet none sought peacefulness for mankind more earnestly, and Moulana recited:

'Man is made of clay; and
If there may not be clay;
With what would a man be fashioned?'

Here the allusion to 'clay' is meant that clay and earth are always 'below' and not above; such as the air, and light and atmosphere; and, therefore, clay is situated in a 'humbler position' and remains in a humbler position, not like fire that rises up with pride and arrogance. The point being that as man is created from clay, he should always be in control of his Ego: and not hold himself up with arrogance and pride of place; thus humbleness is both a natural station of human beings and a virtue. This humbleness, however, does not mean self-effacement, for individuality must be preserved; as the tall trees preserve their height; but height alone is not virtue; therefore, to add to the height and add fruit to the height, humbleness is enjoined in Sufi behaviour both in thought and action.

COURTESY

It is also narrated that another characteristic of Moulana was that he was very fond of little children and very old women; and gave extra thought to them, showing courtesy and love to them. He carried this practice towards everyone, irrespective of religious association or race or station in life; and treated them even with respect; for instance, once a very aged Christian Armenian woman crossed his path. Seeing her bent form, Moulana stopped and bared his head before her in respect, and bowed towards her seven times; whereupon the aged woman did the same towards the master sage.

It is narrated also that Moulana used to show the utmost politeness to little children and old women, even if they were not of the faith, and used to bless them; thus it was that one day an Armenian by the name of Tumbal ('lazy') crossed his path, and Moulana showed a very respectful attitude towards him, and he saluted him seven times, so did Moulana an equal number of times.

Likewise, it is narrated that one day Moulana was passing through a street, and saw a group of children there at play; who, seeing Moulana, ran up to him and saluted him, to which Moulana responded with affection. One small child seeing Moulana and not having joined the group, shouted that they might wait until he arrived. Moulana awaited the small urchin's convenience.

People used to accuse Moulana of having strayed from the Right Path in his mystical practices; and strongly objected to the plays and song and music of his meetings; but to all these objections Moulana said nothing, and these objectors have disappeared from the scene of life as if they never have been; whereas the teachings of Moulana will remain to the end of Time.

It is also narrated that, one day a disciple held a meeting of spiritual song in honour of Moulana; and Moulana, upon arriving at the gateway of his host, waited until everyone had entered, then Moulana entered the house; and the meeting was held with great effect and zest; and Moulana stayed the night at his host's house; who greatly rejoiced that such a Master had honoured him.

The saintly Hisamuddin had asked why Moulana waited outside until everybody else had gone in; to which he replied that he did so because if he had gone in first, then the gatekeepers would have stopped others from entering the house out of respect to him.

His poorer disciples would thus have been prevented from having access to him and profiting from his preaching and prayers. He added that if he could not get his poorer disciples entry into the houses of his rich disciples, how could he hope to gain admittance for such men with little material influence into paradise? What he actually meant was that in this life where materialism is predominant, men are measured according to their wealth and riches; and that men with less wealth if not admitted to his meetings because these men were poor, would be deprived of the blessings of prayer and devotion to be performed at his meetings and at which these poor men could not take a part — if they, thus, did not take part, it is obvious that their chances of admittance to paradise would be less. Moulana, therefore, gave a chance to these poorer elements of his fraternity to gain virtue by joining him in prayer and devotional audition-meetings; and waited for them to enter the hall of the rich man first, fearing that if he went in first, the door would be shut and the poorer people would not be allowed in. The disciples, appreciating the consideration given to the humblest of them by Moulana, thanked him greatly.

FORGIVENESS

It is also related that one day Moulana had sent a recommendation to a noble disciple, the Parwana, to forgive a man who had committed a murder; to which the man replied saying that the matter was beyond his competence; and Moulana wrote back to say that a man who commits a murder is one who takes a life; and he is to be called the son of Azrael — the angel of death, who takes people's lives. Therefore, the Moulana argued, such a man being the son of such an one cannot but take life, for that is his function. The other was amused by the argument and allowed that the man might be released if the murdered person's relatives would accept compensation. Here it by no means signifies that Moulana in any way condoned such crimes, but it is an indication that he pointed to the fact that a person can be released by law if his relatives are satisfied with blood-money; an accepted rule of law of the time and place.

THE INWARD EYE

It is also narrated that Moulana Shamsuddin Malti
reported that one day Moulana was giving a discourse of
mystical subjects at the Seminary, when he said that he
loved Shamsuddin much, but he had one fault; and then
Shamsuddin begged to be enlightened as to what that fault
was; and Moulana said 'Whatever he (Shamsuddin)
perceives and sees, he thinks that God's most blessed thing
and God's most blessed person is that thing or that person';
and then Moulana recited these verses:

'As many a man has
The Inwardness of Satan;
Should one hail everyone
As a Saint?

When your Inward Eye
Is opened; —
The Real Master
Can then be perceived!'

THE MARKET PLACE

Thereafter Shamsuddin became a more devoted disciple; and agreed that it was true what Moulana had said, that as he had the urge of a Seeker, he did actually seek the company of every seeming master, but what Moulana said had opened his eyes towards the reality of a true master. On that day Moulana recited the following verse, and ordered all his disciples to commit it to memory. It read:

> In this market-place of
> The Occult medicine-sellers;
> Do not run hither and thither
> To every shop:
>> But rather sit at the booth
>> Of one who has the real remedy to give!

SELF-DECEPTION

It is also narrated that one day Moulana was giving a mystical discourse in relation to the statement of the Great Master Bayazid (Peace be upon his soul) that he acclaimed the Prophet Mohammed not only because of the Prophet's miracle of the Division of the Moon, the Coming together of Trees, or the Voice of the Vegetation; but more especially because of his prohibiting the use of alcohol to his followers; for whosoever performs an act of virtue gains more virtue if he is the first to act in that manner; because if he had seen any benefit in drinking wine he would have done it himself first; but as the Prophet was the Disciple of God he obeyed God, and taught the men of his faith to act likewise; and he recited the following couplet:

> 'If only you might abstain from wine,
> Only a day or two: (that is but a self-deception),
> You will forfeit Heaven's Light,
> In that which is wine;
> Because universally it is bad, and
> Wicked; thus, to all it is rendered forbidden.'

WEALTH AND POVERTY

It is also narrated that those who wrote about the daily happenings at the court of the Prophet Mohammed, have so narrated that one day the Caliph Usman complained to the Prophet that his wealth increased daily beyond measure; despite his giving charity and helping the poor, the volume of his riches did not diminish; and as 'a great deal of wealth does not give repose of mind', continued Usman, 'how am I to get that peace and repose which poverty gives, if this wealth continues to increase?' It is related that the Prophet said in reply 'Go thou, O Usman, and deliberately perform acts of thanklessness for what God has given you, and by so acting, your riches will soon be reduced'.

Usman said that as he had become accustomed to giving charity and helping the poor for so long, he could not adopt another method in his daily activities. Thereupon the Prophet recited a verse of the Quran saying that he who is grateful for God's blessing continues to have his possessions increased; and those who are ungrateful shall be severely punished; thus, in the Holy Book of the Quran for those who are charitable great reward is promised; and that his (the Prophet's) saying is that he who is thankful for

God's blessings gets more and ever more, and the following couplets were recited by Moulana:

> 'Ungratefulness takes thy riches away from
> Thy palm;
> But thanksgiving gets always more,
> And yet more —
> For thou art nearest to God when thou
> Hast placed thy forehead upon the ground,
> As the expression of thankfulness to thy Lord.'

And then the Prophet said to Usman, 'Go thou, O Usman; these riches of thine which increase cannot but continue to increase, for thou art charitable and generous.' Thereupon Usman, in thanksgiving, presented three hundred camels and their accoutrements to the community and the Prophet blessed him. Moulana thereupon referred to his own day and the habits of the then ruler, one named Emir Muinuddin Sulaiman, whom Moulana likened to the Caliph Usman, who helped the Dervishes, the men of learning, the wayfarers, the needy and the ailing; and who ruled over the hearts of his people; who in turn prayed for their ruler; with the consequences that whatever he undertook bore fruit and was successful. One of the disciples, blessed as he was with considerable wealth, was greatly pleased at the praises that Moulana bestowed upon the ruler of that country; and as an expression of his regard and acceptance of Moulana's dictum, he kissed the feet of Moulana and presented two thousand dinars for the relief of less fortunate disciples, to be distributed to the poor and the needy, the learned men and the Dervishes.

THE RADIANCE

It is likewise narrated that Shamsuddin Mualim related that one day Moulana, addressing the disciples, said that the Prophet had said that when the heart of the faithful is filled with the radiance of God, the heart becomes fertile and productive of pious thoughts and reactions. The Prophet was asked how one could discern that the light of God had entered the heart of a man; to which he replied that such a person loses all worldly desires and all pleasures of a worldly nature forfeit their allure so far as he is concerned. And that he becomes a stranger to his friends and relatives, nor has he any expectations from anyone, or desires anything from anybody.

THE AUDIENCE OF DOGS

It is also related that one day Moulana was giving a lecture at a crossroads to all and sundry on mystical matters, and many men had been attracted by his speech; then he turned his face towards the wall of the roadside and went into contemplation. This he continued until sundown; and then he turned his gaze upon a group of stray dogs. The dogs wagged their tails and seemed as if listening in attention; and noting the attention of even the animals, Moulana said: 'By the Greatness of God, By His Mightiness, He, Who has power over everything, and He without Whom there is nothing; these dogs, too, have a capacity of perceiving mystical meaning. After this, do not call them dogs, but of the tribe of that animal which died with the pious man of the Cavern, Kahaf, (meaning the supreme degree of loyalty which the dog of the pious men of Kahaf, the Seven Sleepers, had attained; for he did not desert his masters and died with them in the wilderness for want of food and water). Here the quality of loyalty is enjoined; and the Moulana recited the following:

> 'If the dog's love for his master was
> Not supreme in loyalty;

How could a Dog reach the greatness of
The Pious men's dog in loyalty?
Should a dog belong to that path of loyalty
His every hair is equal to that of a lion.
These walls of the mosque understand the secret,
Better blind the eye that perceives that not.
The walls and the doors realise the truth;
They are not only made of the elements of earth and
Air, and water — as things material.'

In a short time Moulana's many disciples flocked around
him; and he welcomed them saying, 'Come, come, the
beloved has arrived; come, come, the garden has
blossomed!' and they made obeisance to him. Addressing
them on matters of mystical meaning they all wended their
way with him towards the Seminary, when that whole
night the meeting of mystic audition and poems held
session; and in a fit of ecstasy he cried out: 'By God the
Merciful, the solicitude that these men have bestowed
upon saints and pious men, they bestow upon myself —
the humble person — perhaps they do great kindness to
me!'

THE MIRACULOUS KOHL

It is also narrated that Hisamuddin Chalabi, who had received especial training from Moulana, related that one day Moulana stated that God had a certain *kohl* which, when applied to one's eyes, opens the apparent and inward eyes; and he can see the mystery of existence, and know the meaning of hidden things; and He can grant such a *kohl* to one that He pleases; and if such a *kohl* is not vouchsafed, the person never 'sees nor perceives the meaning' of anything; and then Moulana recited the following:

> 'Without God's grace, and the grace of His
>   accepted ones;
> Even if one is a monarch, his luck is blank.
> Without Divine Grace, the eye is dim;
> Without Divine Grace, the knot cannot be untied.'

And then Moulana said: 'From the gaze of a Shiekh, either be illuminated, or then go out of sight,' Then he recited another couplet:

> 'If seekest thou the light,
> Be prepared.
> But if thou only seekest thyself,
> Then "be out of sight".'

MIND-READING

Moulana Sirajuddin tells us that one day he had gone to the garden of Hisamuddin, and from there brought a bunch of flowers; and he thought that Moulana would be in the house of Chalabi. He entered and found that important men of learning were sitting with Moulana, and that Moulana was giving a discourse on the mystic meaning of things; and the disciples were writing notes of that discourse; and, 'I forgot the bunch of flowers wrapped as it was in my hankerchief', he continued. 'Moulana', said Sirajuddin, 'turned his face towards me, and observed that whosoever comes from a garden should bring flowers with him, as whosoever comes from the shop of a sweets-seller is expected to bring back with him some sweets.' Sirajuddin was amazed by that remark; and paying respects to Moulana, placed the flowers before him; and thereupon mystical songs were chanted.

ALL MANKIND

In a like manner it is narrated that in the house of Sheikh Sirajuddin once Moulana explained that all members of the entire creation share in the existence of one another — and nothing exists singly and unattached — so that when it was said in prayer by the Prophet 'O God guide the people, for they know not', Moulana observed that by the word 'people' is meant the whole of mankind, for if 'the unit' is not itself united, it cannot make a 'whole', meaning that all are interdependant; and he recited the couplet:

> 'All — all
> Are related
> To one another and to a Darwesh.
> If it not be so.
> How can a Darwesh be?'

SPECIAL MYSTICAL PROJECTION

Likewise it is narrated that one day Moinuddin requested the son of Moulana whether he could ask his father 'to give Moinuddin especial mystical projection'. Moulana's son conveyed the request to his father; who replied that the bucket which forty men drink cannot be quaffed by one person; which means that one man cannot bear the impact of mystical force; and forty persons can sustain the impact, and one person could not hold and support the refulgence of 'mystical light' because of the great power of that light. His son offered his thanks and said he could not have known this, if he had not asked the favour on behalf of the disciple.

PARABLE OF THE FRUIT-TREES

It is also narrated that one day a disciple approached the son of Moulana, saying that the entire learned populace of Qonia were anxious to hear and to profit by the preaching of Moulana, and would he request Moulana to address them. To which Moulana replied with acceptance and observed that these persons who addressed themselves to that request were worthy, like the fruit-laden trees whose branches overloaded with fruit hang down in humbleness, so that they might profit by their fruits. Humility had given them grace of mind; they were not like those whose branches had risen to the highest point in the skies in 'self-pride, and self-seeking, and thus without fruitfulness', and that if they had been so they would not have invited him to address them.

MEMORY AND ACTION

It is reported from the saintly son of Moulana that one day one Emir known as Moinuddin requested Moulana to give him some advice so that he might profit by it as a ruler of men. For a short time Moulana held his peace, and then said: 'O Emir, I hear that you have committed the Holy Quran to memory.' To which the Emir replied in the affirmative. Again Moulana asked whether the Emir had learned the entire Traditions of the Prophet from the learned Sheikh Sadruddin; and the Emir replied that that was the case; whereupon Moulana said to the ruler, 'You know the Commandments of God through His Holy Book of the Quran, and know too, the sayings of the Prophet; and from them you have not gained wisdom, and do not act upon the injunctions contained therein. You now ask me to give you advice; how can you act upon that when (greater authorities) remain unobeyed in your mind?' The man wept and asked for the forgiveness of God; and thereafter acted with justice, and became charitable and became famous for his piety; and Moulana asked for the mystical recitations to be made.

THAT WHICH IS APPARENT AND THAT WHICH IS HIDDEN

It is also narrated that once the learned men of the town who were envious of Moulana's prestige, approached the Grand Qadi saying that certain practices of song and mystical dance as performed at the Seminary of Moulana were unorthodox; and in any case, they desired to know the depth of knowledge of that mystic master in matters of real learning — as perceived by the ordinary senses of man. The Grand Qadi advised the dissenters to leave well alone, for in learning of that 'which is apparent and that which is hidden' Moulana had no compeer; but the others insisted that the attainments of Moulana must be tested; so several 'Question Papers' were evolved for Moulana to answer; the questions ranged over all known sciences; such as mathematics, philosophy, astronomy, metaphysics, literature, poetry, logic, law and others. These papers were sent to Moulana through a Turkish messenger; who found Moulana sitting and studying a book at the moat near the Sultan's gateway. After the usual salutations, the bearer gave the papers to Moulana, and waited. Moulana asked for pen and ink to be brought; and wrote the replies to each question with such thoroughness and depth of knowledge, giving all the necessary references, that when the paper bearing the answers was received by those who awaited it, they were astounded by the completeness of the replies and were utterly humbled.

In regard to the validity of the playing of musical instruments — especially the Rubab (the viol) — in the light of orthodoxy, Moulana's replying was complete and convincing; so that he would not let the opportunity pass, but wrote on the back of the long reply a statement in praise of the Rubab — as an instrument whose sound and music aided the esoteric atmosphere — adding that the playing thereof was to help his mystical friends in the realm of concentration; and he had taken to this life of guidance to help his people, and not for any other reason; for to help others was the task of true 'lovers of piety' and recited the couplet saying:

> 'Knowst thou what sings the Rubab?
> Shedding tears with heart athrob!'

The dissenters, feeling 'repulsed' and in shame, sought forgiveness from the Grand Qadi; and five of them became devoted disciples of Moulana forthwith; for they had now been convinced that Moulana's learning was complete in every way.

MIRACLE OF THE PILGRIMAGE

It is also related that a group of people who had returned from a pilgrimage to Mecca, upon reaching Qonia, were going around seeing men of learning and piety; and they also came to visit Moulana. They still wore the Pilgrim's garb — the *Ahram*. When they entered the house, and saw Moulana sitting in the archway, they in one voice raised a cry — *Allahu Akbar*: Allah is Great — in utter astonishment upon beholding Moulana and were so overwhelmed that they fainted. When they came to, the disciples asked the reason thereof; and the pilgrims said: 'Of a truth this very person (Moulana, wearing the same clothes) was with us in all the ceremonies of the pilgrimage, and gave us instructions from time to time in our prayers, and conducted us to the Tomb of The Prophet at Medina; although he never travelled with us from this city, nor ate nor slept with us.' This is a well known mystical experience in Sufi Lore, when a Great Sufi can be in two places at one and the same time.

It is likewise narrated that one of the merchants of the town was a devoted disciple of Moulana, who went on a pilgrimage to Mecca. When the time of the pilgrimage was terminating, the wife of the pilgrim-merchant prepared some sweets and distributed them to the poor and to relatives as a thanksgiving for her absent pilgrim husband. A quantity of sweets was sent to Moulana, who invited other disciples to partake of it, and also to keep a portion for themselves as a token of the day. The disciples helped themselves as much as they could, and yet there was no finishing the sweets; and then the Moulana took the plate upstairs to the flat roof of the seminary and called out — to no one in sight — to 'take his share'. Upon descending to where the disciples were sitting, he said, when he came down without the large tray of sweets, that he had sent a share to the merchant, who was at the time on a pilgrimage at Mecca. Quite naturally, this action mystified the disciples.

When the merchant returned home after performing his pilgrimage, he came to pay his respects to Moulana; who was pleased to hear from the pilgrim that all was well in his house. When, later, the servants of the pilgrim merchant were unpacking the effects of the returned traveller, his wife saw the tray among his things, and marvelled at it, and asked how that tray got into his luggage. The merchant said that one day when he was in the camp outside Mecca, and was with other pilgrims, he saw that tray full of sweets pushed through the curtain of his tent; and the owner of the hand that had pushed in the tray could not be found: despite the fact that the servants ran out to see who was the bearer of the tray. Both the husband and the wife, marvelling at this manifestation of Moulana, went to him and made their further allegiance to the master; whereupon Moulana observed that all this was due to their faithfulness towards him, so that God in His Greatness had enabled him to perform that wonderful action.

THE LAST DISCOURSE

It is also narrated that on a Friday after the prayer, Moulana was giving a great sermon, when one who had acquired some knowledge of religious lore observed that there are, of course, some who prepare their sermons on given subjects and having committed to memory certain verses of the Quran quote those verses to impress their audience; but the other class consists of those true scholars who could deliver a discourse upon any verse that might be quoted.

Moulana, having heard the remark, asked the man to recite any verse of the Quran upon which a discourse might be required; and the man thereupon recited the verse of *Ad Duha* which runs as follows:

> 'Consider the early hours of the Dawn,
> and the night when it covers with darkness...'

Moulana gave such a remarkable discourse on the verse that everyone was moved to the utmost degree, and the discourse lasted until the evening prayer from the early afternoon, showing that Moulana was master of the lore of Koranic exegesis. The questioner was silenced and went into ecstasy along with others who heard the masterful interpretation; and kissing the foot of the dais where sat the Master he begged to be enrolled into the ranks of the disciples. It is often said that that was the last discourse of Moulana, but others do not agree, and say that Moulana lived much after that date.

REMEMBERING DEATH

It is also narrated that in those times an important man of Qonia had died, and Moulana was present among the mourners, though he stayed outside the house where the death had occurred; awaiting the coffin to be brought out and taken in procession to the graveyard. Kamaluddin stood at the gateway of the house of the deceased and saluted those who came to join the procession; and when at last the coffin was to be lowered into the grave Moulana, standing at the side of the grave, asked that they should hear the funeral oration, and summoned Kamaluddin also; then he said, 'Supposing one Sadruddin and another Badruddin (who had departed) were to be asked to present themselves out of their graves, one could not say whether either had the "radiance and blessings of God" upon them as the records of the Recording Angels would be first read to them; as all those who "go-away" go with their good deeds or evil actions with them, thus it is necessary to remember the Day of Judgement, as this dead person will also be judged according to his actions.'

The object-lesson thus conveyed to those who heard him on that occasion made a profound effect. Kamaluddin, the nearest relative of the deceased, became unconscious with the impact of Moulana's address; and many of those who were still unbelievers came forward and became disciples of Moulana.

AT THE HOT SPRINGS

It is also recorded that it was the custom of the Moulana that every winter he used to go to a riverside where flowed a hot spring, for forty or fifty days. In that spot Moulana used to deliver occult lectures to his disciples. During some of these discourses the ducks in the river used to make a noise and disturb the lectures; then one day Moulana called out to the ducks to be silent and said to them, that either they should speak or that he might be permitted to do so. Immediately the birds became silent, and the lectures continued; and when ultimately, he struck camp, he came forward to the bank of the river and said to the ducks that they could thenceforward make such noise as they pleased, with the consequence that the birds started making their usual noises.

THE COW TAKES REFUGE
FROM THE BUTCHERS

It is also narrated that on one occasion the butchers of the town, having bought a cow, were going to slaughter her; but the cow chewed her rope until it parted, and ran out into the streets, and the butchers ran after her trying to capture the animal. But the fleet-footed cow could not be caught, and a whole group of people chased her from street to street. It so happened that Moulana was walking through a street, and the cow made straight for the master, and stopped.

Moulana stroked the animal, and she stood submissive, making no effort to run away. The butchers, coming upon the scene, were relieved to know that the animal was now caught, and giving their salutations expected that the cow would be handed over to them. But Moulana's resolve was different. He told the butchers not to kill the cow, but to leave the fugitive alone; for she had taken refuge with him. They obeyed the master; and Moulana thereupon observed 'Since even dumb animals can be rescued by men who "love God" how much more could human beings be rescued and placed on the right path by following a Man-of-God.' This saying so affected the disciples that they felt the presence of a mystical influence, and esoteric audition was started, when the hearers gave their shirts to the singers in ecstasy; and it is further reported that that cow was never again seen in Qonia.

WHICH WAY LIES THE PATH

It is also narrated that Sheikh Sinanuddin Najjar, who was one of the great disciples, reported that once Moulana said that the lovers of God are annihilated and 'absorbed' in the zest of divine love; and those who love things that perish — as all matter must perish, and all sons and wives must die and all things created must cease to exist save the Face of God — likewise a man is 'absorbed' and is annihilated into those things of matter and ceases to exist.

God has created all that is from a nothingness, and to nothingness it must all return. During the same meeting Moulana is stated to have observed when he heard the voice of a wandering Darwesh, whether it was a voice or was it the echo of things of the world — a perishable world? At that meeting, too, Qutbuddin asked what was the Path of Moulana; and received the reply that his way was to die — like everybody else — and to take the benefit of one's actions to the high heavens — for reward or punishment — as the case might be. For Moulana further said that unless one 'dies' — or is master of his desires and controls them and purifies himself, he never reaches the right destination; and then Qutbuddin cried and asked which way he was to proceed; and Moulana recited the following verse to him:

'I asked for the path —
Seek thou, he replied.
   Again, I asked,
   Pray, what way lies the Path?
He said:
   Follow on and seek.
   Then turning to me,
He said:
   O thou Seeker — thy quest is long
   All the while, seek and seek again.'

Qutbuddin was moved beyond measure, and became an accepted disciple of the Moulana forthwith.

MOTHER EARTH

It is also narrated that when one of the major disciples had died, his compatriots discussing as to whether he was to be put in the grave in a wooden coffin or without it and not arriving at a decision asked the advice of the saint Karamuddin. He gave his opinion that the body was to be interred without the wooden coffin; for he explained that as a mother loves her offspring more than the love of a brother thus the mother earth will hold her son more fondly in her lap than the wood of the coffin, for the wood is created from earth and therefore a 'brother creation'. When Moulana heard of this decision, he complimented the saint; and said that he had never seen this explanation in any book.

ADMIT THY WORK...

It is also narrated that the Grand Qadi and the Head of the Administration, one named the celebrated Kamaluddin, who was the highest legal authority in the land, went to Qonia. Having seen the Governor, one named Izuddin Kaykaoos, he took advantage of his presence in that town to meet learned men of the locality, such as Shumsuddin and Zeenuddin Razi, and Shumsuddin Malti. And he stated that many of these men of learning and piety impressed upon him the necessity of meeting Moulana; and he, therefore, sought a time to see that great personage.

'As soon as I entered Moulana's house,' said the Grand Qadi, 'I was benumbed with the magnificence of the visage of that great Sage; and Moulana rose to receive me with great courtesy and affection; and welcomed me by saying:

"Thou desertest us, admit thy work;
Seest thou not, how we capture thy attention!" '

and then Moulana observed that thanks to God the Qadi had attained that greatness of learning and prestige; and had so contributed to learning and piety. 'And then Moulana started on a discourse of such lofty ideas,' added the Grand Qadi, 'the like of which I had never heard nor read; and having been mightily impressed, I, together with my son and Atabek and a few other important persons became disciples of Moulana. When I returned to my residence, I felt the "draw" of the Moulana, and felt uneasy unless I went to the presence of that Great Master; and arranged that a great meeting of mystical music should be given to honour my Master; and, therefore, I invited a very large number of important men of learning of the town of Qonia at that occasion.

'As the number of the persons invited was very large, large-scale arrangements had to be made; and especially for cool drinks we could not muster more than thirty large cauldrons, and we procured a few cones of sugar to make sherbet and,' continued the Grand Qadi, 'I had to ask the First Lady: the Governor's wife, to lend us some more large vessels for the purpose, as we had to entertain a considerable number of people. I planned to make a special cool drink of honey for especial guests; and, thinking that the thirst of many had to be quenched, I was wondering whether we had enough for the purpose. But, lo, and behold, I saw Moulana enter the house — as if from nowhere, and solve the problem by saying that we should just add more water to that which was present; and saying this, he "disappeared" and the servants and others ran out to find him — but there was no trace of him anywhere. Acting thus on the advice given, we poured the whole lot of sherbet into the metal tank of the mosque and simply added more and yet more water; and I told the servants to taste the water from time to time and take care that too much water was not added; but a wonder of all wonders so occurred that the more water that was added, the sweeter the sherbet in the tank became! We continued to put in more and yet more water, till we felt that the limit had been reached; and we were all staggered by the "miracle" of Moulana.

'However, from the late afternoon till midnight the mystical musical ceremonies continued with unprecedented ecstasy amongst all the guests; and I and Moinuddin were plying the guests with the cool drink the whole time; and Moulana recited the following poem:

"Love's warming breath aleaping —
As fragrance of Love wafts on;
To all the Learned release anon.
The Liquid of Life — the Life Eternal."

'As the song of mystery gathered momentum, and we were in a frenzy of mystical movement, Moulana pulled me to his side in affection and kissed me on both cheeks, and then read a verse from his ode saying:

"If thou knowest me not —
Ask the sleepless nights,
Ask my tired face,
And my parched lips in anguish
For the separation from the Beloved."

'Many fell to their knees, kissing Moulana's feet and begging to become his disciples; and my worldly goods increased and my love for the mystical vision was augmented to a great stage of "Refinement" and feelings came to my mind, which beggar description as the Arabic saying goes: "Sometimes what is in the heart cannot come to the lips", and I said so and became a "servant-disciple" and was blessed and a door of twin greatness was opened to me.'

THE WONDER OF THE CANDLES

Likewise it is reported that one day Moinuddin held a mystical audition-meeting to which he invited many dignitaries of the town. Each of these men brought large-sized candles as their contribution to the illuminations of the meeting; and to the astonishment of all Moulana carried the smallest possible candle. None said anything, but side-glances of amazement were exchanged; for some attributed the fact to miserliness, whilst others frankly thought that Moulana was mad. All this was not lost upon Moulana, who ultimately observed that his small candle was really the 'life-sap' of all the giant candles brought by others. Those who were friendly to Moulana agreed with him, but many others dissented; whereupon Moulana said: 'If you do not believe what I say, you can have the proof'; and saying that 'acting'; for, lo, the whole hall was plunged into darkness — for Moulana had extinguished his own little candle. Then the Master lit his candle again, with the result that all other large candles came to life again automatically: to the utter bewilderment and amazement of all. The non-believers acknowledged their mistake and then the mystic audition swelled anew with great force; so that the meeting lasted the entire night — all the larger candles having been used up, the little candle of the Master still burned as before, losing none of its lustre or its substance. Many became Moulana's disciples that day.

THE MEANING OF POSSESSIONS

It is also narrated that the great man of learning and the famous Head of the School of Theology at Qasaria, who was invited to become a teacher at a newly-created college, was one of the important disciples of the Sage. He reports that the Master once observed that it was not permitted to offer prayers, when the Master was still in 'congregation' — in a mystical gathering. When the Master was in that state and the disciples were immersed in that atmosphere of 'divine' aura, some, leaving the circle, started to offer prayers. Moulana's listening to the mystical music and being wrapped in the mystic-state was as offering the prayer or keeping fast during the month of fasting amongst the Muslims; so Moulana added.

'. . . And when holding a mere particle of the radiance of the Prophet Mohammed, I say that Godliness is nothing other than being enraptured in the Divine Love. I am enveloped in that atmosphere of alienation from things material, so that my very being is lit with the ecstasy and happiness of other-than-worldliness; so that my disciples should share with me that radiance by listening to me, and by being in contact with me. When, therefore, you find such a one, consider it a singular mark of good fortune, and make your body and soul radiant with my association and be thankful for such a contact.'

Moulana further observed that one should not get involved in useless discussions as to what is the right vocation to follow and what is the nature of possessions; for the real thing is the manner in which such possessions are spent. 'If, therefore,' said Moulana, 'it gives the feeling of being enmeshed in mere materialistic ends without a soul to it, then — however legitimately such a possession is got — it is "unlawful" and base and mean. Eat your bread in such a way that the bread does not become your master; and as the Prophet said in this respect about the Caliph Omar: "Eat thou thy bread like Omar: people give him bread and he serves the people",' and further in this connection Moulana recited the following couplets:

'Not less than jewels a morsel if,
When taken for divine service's sake.
As morsel at last may become refuse,
Its foul smell do not let escape
    In foul deeds and more —
Then rather lock thy mouth —
    And lose the key!
With whose morsel piety is mixed
    His means of morsel are all morally good.'

THE PERCEIVING EYE

It is likewise narrated that one Shamsuddin, the learned Teacher, used to gaze fixedly at the face of Moulana all the time during the mystical chants; and when Moulana asked why he did not join in during the performance, the disciple replied that he saw no-one more worthy to be looked at and nothing gave him greater pleasure than gazing at the visage of his master. The Master observed that he welcomed such a sentiment, but his face had also another face — an inward facet — which the disciple ought to concentrate upon and see the divine perception in it of the Light of God's mysteries. He added that it is not always desirable to stare at the blazing sun, for that intensity of light might dazzle the sight to the extent that one would not be able to see again; and merely gazing at the outward aspect might not give 'sight' to the inward eye, and then Moulana recited the following:

'O, thou of Perceiving Eye!
   Repose alone.
     Only in His Reflected rays,
    Never daring to stare
    At the Visage of His Mighty Grace.'

(Here it should be noted that Moulana neither here nor at any other place in this text claims any Divine attributes to himself, but in mystical terms, a man's being is at one supreme stage, so 'annihilated' that the mystic sees and feels nothing but God and his Divine attributes 'in him and about him'; and literally 'he is in this world of matter but not of it', as is often said in mystical writings.)

SEEING THE EVIL IN THE MAN OF LEARNING

It is also related that the pious reported Bahauddin once asked Moulana what was that 'evil practice' to which the Sheikhs are given, according to the vulgar people of the market. To which Moulana replied: 'That "evil practice" is surely known to all, but it is committed in secret; but most certainly those Sheikhs, who are Dervishes do not possess that evil habit; but those who parade in the garb of holy men, and are not pious inwardly, in time develop the evil habit, and their learning hides their ungodly habit though ultimately they are exposed and condemned.'

Such, for instance, was the case of a great man of learning, but of little piety, who used to challenge such learned men as Sadruddin; and he had gathered an influential following. One day it so happened that Moulana was passing the neighbourhood where this man, known as Nasiruddin, lived, and he was sitting in the balcony of his great house surrounded by his disciples; and he saw Moulana and said: 'How strange is the face of that man, and look at his turban and dress; and I do not know whether he has any spark of mystical attainments in his heart; and what kind of man would be his successor.'

Moulana passed beside the wall of that Sheikh's mighty

castle, and looking up said: 'O thou of little manners, beware!' Instantly, Nasiruddin the Sheikh shrieked, as if stung, and fell on his knees in pain; and his disciples ran round and anxiously enquired the reason thereof, and he replied that he had uttered a mouthful of ungracious remarks about Moulana, and he did not know how great was the mystical power of that master. On the other hand, those who were with Moulana at the time did not know to whom his remarks were directed, until he enlightened them, and the whole thing spread throughout the bazaars and streets. Soon the people began to gossip and it was revealed that the learned Sheikh was of ill-repute morally and gave money to people to advertise his name and proclaim his sanctity, and 'so hidden were his evil ways', that the people believed in him. Ultimately he was condemned by everyone in Qonia, and at last his disciples gave him a drug to release themselves from association from an evil person masquerading as a holy man.

DOGS AND MEN

It is also narrated that Sheikh Badruddin the great artist, reported that one day he and the headmaster of the school, Sirajuddin, were walking with Moulana, when Moulana said to them that he really wanted to walk alone, for he was tired of the salutations and expressions of respect that people gave him wherever he went, and he wanted to be alone. He walked alone for a while, until he saw a pack of dogs on the sandy patch of the environs of the towns; and the headmaster coming near Moulana, drew his attention to the peace and contentment that pervaded the group of dogs as they lay in repose in the sunshine. 'Look at these dogs, how united and friendly they are towards each other; and we human beings?'

Moulana reflected a bit and then said, 'Of a truth, it is so, that these dogs lie in repose and peace now, but throw a bone amongst them, and then see the disturbance of the unity of which you speak. It is so with mankind,' continued Moulana, 'men, as long as there is selflessness between two people and the gain of worldly things is not considered amongst them, they are the best of friends; but let greed of the world be thrown before them, then note how the peace is disturbed and fighting, worse than dogs', ensues.' Only those who set little store upon the passing things of matter and of possessing that which must 'die and perish' can have a peaceful and reposeful life.

THE COINS OF GOLD

It is also narrated that once Moinuddin, the disciple, invited Moulana to a mystical meeting, at which important men of the town were also invited in his honour. After the listening was over, food was served, and an especial dish was placed before Moulana containing some very tasty food. Moinuddin had placed in the dish a purse full of gold coins and had hidden it well in a heap of rice on the plate. This was done to test whether Moulana would notice it without touching the food. The host, as a further ruse, insisted that the food might graciously be taken, and he added that the food was bought from money legitimately earned. But Moulana sat without touching the food; and then observed that good food should not be contaminated by such things as gold coins — he had 'discovered' the ruse, obviously through inner powers; and then he recited the first verse of a long ode:

> 'My heart bears love to neither
>   Matter's sweetest things,
>   Nor their gloss and glow!
> Thus, forsooth;
>   No golden purse for me
>   In the dying matter's precious bowl.'

The host begged forgiveness of Moulana; and touched the Master's feet in salutation and in expressions of 'shame for testing his master'.

THE HIDDEN DERVISH

It is also narrated that once the son of Moulana asked his father what was meant by the statement that the true Dervish is always 'hidden' — or, to say it in different words, he keeps himself 'concealed'; whether that statement meant that he disguises himself by clothing, or is it a mental attitude of mind?

Moulana's reply was this: 'It might be both: even in adopting a vocation to hide the real pursuit of the Path; for instance', continued Moulana, 'some saints write verses depicting love — and that love people take as carnal love — others, engaged in trade (such as Baba Fariddudin Attar, who was a chemist and had a chemist's shop in a bazaar); others concentrate upon writing on literary matters; and yet another might pursue other callings. All these are designed to 'conceal' what they really are. This they do to avoid becoming the subject of 'pestering' by worldly persons. There is another set of them who deliberately perform actions of which society might disapprove, so that people of worldly mind might leave them alone; and thus it is said that the Prophet has said that 'Allah has hidden the true "Men of Great Piety".' Every device is, therefore, resorted to, to find peace of mind by such persons to follow the Path, which is hindered by contamination with worldly ones — people whose sole aim and purpose is to gain material ends at whatever cost. That cost is the mystical and spiritual sphere and activity and love of that Who Is Always, and Will Be Always, and Was Always.' And then Moulana recited the following verses:

'Knowing all the time — all,
    And yet they hide and seek.
To the worldly gaze they appear
    Other than what they really are.

Not for a moment though,
    Many see them, what they are.
In inward light they roam
    Making miracles come to life,
And yet none knowing
    What they are.

Betimes even the Lesser Saints, Abdals,
Know less than what they are:
    Their ins and outs,
    A mystery for all.'

'DIE BEFORE YOUR DEATH...'

It is also narrated that once Moulana said to his son: 'If the people ask you what is your Path, then reply "My Path is to eat very little, nay, my Path is 'to die' that is, to be annihilated into the radiance of the Divine".' And then he related a story of a Dervish who, approaching a house, asked for some water to drink. A very beautiful girl appeared at the door and handed an empty utensil to the man; but the dervish said: 'I want some water to drink.' The girl asked him to go away, saying, 'I have given you your reply, for a Dervish is not one who eats the whole day and sleeps the whole night; but the real pious one is he who sleeps hungry many a night and eats nothing during the day.' Another Persian sage has said: 'Eating is to preserve life, not living only to eat and yet eat more.' Moulana said that the Dervish, after that encounter with the girl, never ate during the day until his last hour.

SIMILAR EFFECTS MUST HAVE SIMILAR CAUSES

A shopkeeper kept a parrot in his shop.

One day a cat overturned a vessel of oil and fled.

When the merchant came back, he thought that the bird had spilt the oil, and he struck him so hard that all the feathers fell from his head.

Some time later, seeing a bald man passing by, the parrot called out:

'What oil did *you* spill?'

GIVE ME THE WHOLE,
NOT THE PARTS...

A man went to a tattooist, asking him to put the picture of a lion on his skin.

But this man was a coward. When he felt the first prick, he said:

'Which part of the lion are you drawing?'

The tattooist said: 'The tail.'

The man cried: 'Let us not have a tail, do another part.'

The artist did as he was told. But the man screamed with pain again.

And this went on and on, until the artist told him that it was impossible to tattoo a lion at all, if he would not allow any of its parts to be drawn.

THE KING AND THE SLAVE-GIRL

There was once a king who fell in love with a slave-girl. He bought her, but she became ill, and no doctor could cure her, because every one who tried was too self-willed, and all omitted to say: 'God willing' when they tried their cures.

One day the king dreamt that someone would come to help, and a stranger presented himself at the palace and offered to treat the girl.

When the strange doctor sat beside the patient he realised that the arrogance of the doctors had prevented them from seeing her inner state.

He realised that she was languishing because she was in love. He found out by indirect conversation that she was in love with a certain jeweller of Samarkand.

'To produce a cure' he told the king privately, 'you must attract the goldsmith with a promise of gifts.'

The king sent flatterers to lure the smith. He came, full of greed, and the two were married.

In six months the girl had recovered.

But the strange doctor then administered a certain drink to the goldsmith, and he became repulsive to the girl.

He died, and at the same time the girl's feelings evaporated.

This story shocks you because you do not know the whole of the picture...

THE LOVERS...

The Caliph said to Laila:

'How can Majnun be distracted with you, since you are not more beautiful than many other women?'

'Hold your tongue' she said, 'for you are not Majnun.'

The more wakeful a man is to the things which surround him, the more asleep is he, and his waking is worse than his sleep.

THE STOLEN SNAKE

A man stole a snake from a man who had caught it.

The snake bit him, and he died.

In this way the first man was spared the snake's bite.

The second man had his desire (to steal the snake) but the effect of his wish being granted was to kill him.

JESUS AND THE NAME

A man walking with Jesus saw some bones.

He asked Jesus to teach him how to restore the dead to life.

Jesus said: 'This is not for you. You have not cared about yourself, but you are interested in the reconstituting of another.'

THE SUFI AND THE DONKEY

A Sufi traveller was the guest of some other Sufis. They entertained him well, and he asked their servants to look after his donkey.

He told the servants in such detail what to do with the donkey, how to groom and feed him, that they were annoyed, and said that they needed no such admonitions.

This did not stop the Sufi, who continued to insist, again and again, what they were to do for the ass.

That night he slept badly because he was dreaming that something was happening to his donkey.

In the morning he set off on the animal, but it soon collapsed, because it had not after all been cared for at all by the negligent servants, in spite of the protestations.

> (He thought that he could not trust them, and he was right. They thought that they were too good to need lecturing, and they were wrong.)

THE OLD WOMAN
AND THE HAWK

A hawk belonging to a king ran away to the house of an old woman.

She had never seen a hawk before, and thought that its beak — being curved and long — was deformed. She imagined that its wings were too long. She tried to look after it from her own experience of birds.

The king ultimately found the hawk, and told it that this fate had happened to him because he had chosen the abode of an ignorant crone, however well-meaning, rather than the company of one who knew what a hawk was.

THE SAGE AND THE HALWA

A certain Sufi sage spent money like water on good deeds, without regard for where it came from, and he was therefore always in debt.

At length, when he was on his deathbed, the people to whom he owed money gathered around him, demanding repayment.

The sage heard a sweetmeat-seller in the street crying his wares, and sent out for the whole stock of halwa from the boy.

This was distributed among the creditors. When the time came to pay for it, the Sufi said that he had no money, and was in any case on the point of death.

The boy was utterly distressed, and cursed all Sufis and their ways.

This incident made the creditors commiserate with the boy and increase the virulence of their bitter reproaches to the Sufi as a villain.

The Sufi sage took no notice of any of this. Time passed.

Later in the day a large sum of money, sufficient to repay all the debts, arrived as a donation from one of the Sheikh's admirers.

The Sheikh explained, when the repentant creditors asked him to teach them the meaning of this, that the money would never have appeared as a result of the desires and needs of the lenders. The whole result had to await the genuine heartcry of the halwa-seller's boy.

THE COW AND THE LION

A man once put a cow into a shed. A lion came along, ate up the cow, and took its place.

The shed was dark when the man went back, so he felt his way. His hands touched every part of the lion, and he thought that he was touching his own domestic animal.

The lion thought:

'He would not stroke me if he really knew who I was. He does this only because it is dark, and because he imagines that I must be his tame beast.'

THE SUFI AND THE SERVANT

A Sufi arrived at a settlement of Sufis, and put his donkey in their stables.

The inhabitants were penniless, and they took the animal and sold it.

With the money they bought all kinds of delicacies, and, delighted with their good fortune, they danced and sang.

The visiting Sufi, delighted by their gaiety and welcome of him, joined their revels, crying like them: 'The donkey is gone,' again and again.

The following morning, when the Sufi wanted to go on his way, he found that there was nobody there except his own servant. He asked him to bring his donkey.

The servant explained that the Sufis had taken the donkey away.

'Why did you not tell me, since you were in charge of it?' demanded the Sufi.

'I went frequently to tell you, but each time I approached you, you were calling out, "The donkey is gone", so I thought that you already knew what had happened to it,' his servant explained.

The Sufi realised that his imitative behaviour had been the cause of his loss.

THE BANKRUPT AND THE CAMEL

A certain man was an incorrigible bankrupt.

Because he went about gaining credit from people who did not realise that his credit was not good, the magistrate of his town ordered that he should be conveyed through all the streets while his peculiarity and the danger of trusting him was proclaimed aloud.

The camel of a Kurdish wood-seller was taken away from him, upon which they mounted the bankrupt for the whole day, while the magistrate's decision was cried through the town.

For the whole day the Kurd followed the procession while the situation was called out in various languages for all to understand.

When this had been done, and the bankrupt dismounted at length, the Kurd demanded from him some compensation for the use of the camel.

'What have you been doing all day?' asked the bankrupt, 'if you have not been listening to what everyone has said, that I never pay for anything which I have used.'

THE THIRSTY MAN
AND THE WATER

A thirsty man came to the side of a stream.

He could not reach the water, for there was a wall which he could not negotiate.

He took a brick from the wall, and threw it into the water, so that it made a noise, delicious to his ears. He continued to do this, brick after brick, until people asked him why.

He said:

'There are two reasons. The first is that I enjoy the splashing sound, which is music to the ears of the thirsty. The second reason is that, with each brick I tear off the wall, I get nearer to the level of the water.'

The thirstier the man is, the more he pines for the very sound of the water, and the more and the faster he tears the bricks from the wall.

THE INSANE BEHAVIOUR
OF DHUN'NUN

Dhun'Nun was behaving in what was considered by ordinary people to be such an insane manner that he was taken to an institution for the mad.

Some of his friends went to the madhouse to find out how he was.

They thought that he might have been behaving as he did for deliberate reasons, so that people could learn from him.

When he saw them, he shouted out at them, asking them who they were, and threatening them.

They explained that they were his friends, and that they had come to enquire as to his welfare, and to show that they did not believe that he was really mad.

Dhun'Nun threw sticks and stones at them, and they hurried away from his madness, as they took it to be.

Then Dhun'Nun laughed, and explained:

'They think that they understand that I am only playing the part of a madman, but when they see me doing it, they imagine that I am mad.'

THE SAGE AND THE MAN ASLEEP

A certain man was lying asleep in the open when a dangerous reptile started to enter his mouth.

A sage mounted on a horse saw this happening. He tried to prevent the creature from being swallowed, but he was just too late.

He therefore hit the sleeper a mighty blow to awaken him. Then he mercilessly harried him to a tree under which were rotting fruit.

The horseman forced the man to eat them until he could hold no more.

The man complained and shouted, asking what he had done to be treated in that way.

Now the horseman forced the man to run in front of him until his feet became blistered. This continued until, after many hours, the running man vomited and threw up what he had swallowed. Then it was that he saw the abominable thing which was the real cause of the treatment.

THE BEAR

A man once saved the life of a bear, which became attached to him and grateful for what he had done.

The man, being tired, lay down to sleep, with the bear beside him.

Another man passing by told him to be careful, saying that the friendship of a fool was worse than opposition.

But the first man only thought that the second was jealous of him, and took no notice of these words. He even thought that the other man was trying to deprive him of the security of a faithful companion.

When, however, he lay down to sleep and dozed off, the bear, seeing flies approach, tried to strike them with a stone, and in so doing killed the man who had saved him.

THE GARDENER
AND THE THREE MEN

A gardener saw three men on his land, who should not have been there. They were miscreants: a lawyer, a pretended Sharif (descendant of Mohammed) and a bogus Sufi.

The gardener realised that while these men were united he would not be able to deal with them: they were too strong. So he resolved to cause division among them, so that he could separate them.

He addressed the Sufi, telling him to go to the house to bring a rug for them to sit upon.

The supposed Sufi went off, and the gardener said to the remaining two:

'One of you is a legist, the other a Sharif. Through the pronouncements of the one of you, we are able to eat; and through your learning we can take wing.

'The other is our Prince, a Sovereign, a Prince (Sayed) of the House of the Prophet.

'But who is the greedy, foul Sufi, to be a companion of such important men as you? Oppose him. When he returns, send him away. Then remain in my garden for a week.'

They sent the Sufi away, and the gardener followed him

and struck him with a stick, saying: 'Does Sufihood entitle you to enter my garden?'

The Sufi said to his friends: 'Take care, now, for although you thought badly of me, I am not as bad as this man . . .'

Now that he had dealt with the Sufi, the gardener turned to the Sharif, and said:

'Your Highness, there is food in my house. Go there and ask for it.'

When the Sharif had gone, he spoke to the lawyer.

The gardener told him that he surely realised that the Sharif was a fraud. What he said was a reflection of his own mind, and not true of the descendants of the Prophet. But the lawyer listened to him.

So the gardener was able to approach the Sharif and abuse him, accusing him of theft, asking him what license the Prophet had left for his descendants to rob.

The Sharif said: 'If I am not a Sharif, I am not as bad as you are, for you have surrendered me to this evil man.'

Now the gardener was alone with the lawyer. He said to him:

'Is it your legal judgement that you can steal from me, you thief? What is your statutory authority?'

The lawyer answered:

'You are right, and you may beat me, for this is a correct payment for whoever abandons his friends.'

THE DERVISH WHO
MARRIED A PROSTITUTE

The High Sayed said to the wearer of the dervish robe:

'If you had not been in such a hurry to marry a harlot, and told me of your plans, we would have chosen for you a pure woman.'

The dervish answered:

'I have had nine pure women, and as each of them became loose, I was full of sadness.

'I married this one deliberately, in order to see what would happen. I have attempted reason as far it would go. Now I will practise irrationality.'

THE KING'S HAWK AND THE OWLS

There was once a noble hawk, which belonged to a king. Flying one day the hawk became tired, and settled on a ruined building to rest. The ruin was, however, the home of a colony of owls, who resented his presence.

The owls attacked this noble creature, who told them that he meant no harm, and that he was only passing through their domain.

But the owls cried:

'Do not listen to him! How could he have anything to do with a king? He is lying, in order to deprive us of our home by guile!'

MANIPULATION OF THE MIND

Once upon a time there were some schoolboys. They were lazy and wanted to escape from their studies. One of them suggested that they should make their teacher feel ill by telling him how terrible he looked.

Thus it was that, as soon as the master arrived at the school, one boy after another told him that he was looking ill. At first the teacher told the boys that he was quite well, and they were imagining things; but, as more and more boys, apparently spontaneously, described him as looking ill, he began to feel it himself.

Returning to his house, he told his wife that something was wrong with him. She said that she thought that it was his imagination, but he insisted that he was near to death, and took to his bed, even accusing her of being insensitive to his sufferings.

THE LOVE-POEMS

A lover visiting his beloved brought out the poems which he had written to her, and read them at length. The verses dealt with what he thought of her, and how he felt about her attraction and beauty.

The lady said to him:

'Here you are, with me and able to perceive my qualities directly; but you insist upon expressing emotions which represent yourself, not me.

'I am not your object: it is you who are the object of your own affections. It is you who stand between yourself and me.'

THE KING'S SLAVE

Once upon a time there was a King's slave. This slave was so extremely devoted to the King that he used to faint whenever he entered his presence. Now people knew that this slave was a great favourite of the King's and they would give him all kinds of presents for the King. They would also give him petitions and applications which he would put in his satchel in the hope of presenting them to the King. Yet whenever the slave found himself actually in the King's presence he was so overcome by the King's magnificence and by his devotion to the King, that he used to swoon and collapse on the floor and lie there senseless. When he did so, the King used to pick up the satchel and look in it, he used to take out the presents and read all the petitions and he would act on the petitions and fulfil the wishes of the people who had put them there, although the slave himself had no part at all in the intervention. In this way the slave did not have to put the petitions forward, and the fact that he was in such great awe of the King made really no difference at all.

The King had other slaves and they were also in very great awe of the King. They were so overawed by him that they hardly ever managed to make any petition at all and sometimes when they did manage to and when they did manage to make petitions, hardly any of those were granted.

THE STORY OF
THE LEARNED TEACHER

Once upon a time there was a teacher who knew many things, and he was a very poor man, and even in the coldest weather he only wore a thin shirt. Now a bear had been carried down from the mountains in a river and it was drifting down the river with only its head visible. The pupils of this scholar, knowing that their master didn't have a coat, and seeing only the fur on the bear's head, said to him: 'Look, there's a fur coat in the river and you do need a coat. Why don't you go and get it?' The teacher was very cold and he plunged into the river and caught hold of the skin and the bear caught hold of him, and there he was fighting in the middle of the water.

The pupils shouted: 'Leave it alone and come out,' and the teacher called back to them: 'I've left it but it will not leave me'.

THE STORY OF
THE SEEKER FROM INDIA

A certain seeker from India came to visit a saint and when
he had reached the door of the place where the saint lived, a
voice came from inside saying: 'Go back, you have fulfilled
your purpose and you have profited through having come
to my door.If you actually get to the point of seeing me,
you will lose by it. Similarly a small conversation can carry
a lesson just like a light which kisses a candle and lights it.
That is enough and that has completed the requirement. If
the oven were on fire, if it were so hot as to be on fire, you
would be able to gain no benefit from it. It would be too
much.'